Patrick Miller / Boredom / page 160-163

PUBLISHED BY
PRINCETON ARCHITECTURAL PRESS
37 EAST SEVENTH STREET
NEW YORK, NEW YORK 10003

FOR A FREE CATALOG OF BOOKS, CALL 1.800.722.6657
VISIT OUR WEB SITE AT www.papress.com.

EDITING: JENNIFER N. THOMPSON
DESIGN: MIKE PERRY (www.MIDWESTISBEST.COM)

SPECIAL THANKS TO: NETTIE AIJIAN, SARA BADER, DOROTHY BALL,
NICOLA BEDNAREK, JANET BEHNING, BECCA CASBON, PENNY (YUEN PIK) CHU,
RUSSELL FERNANDEZ, PETE FITZPATRICK, JAN HAUX, CLARE JACOBSON,
JOHN KING, NANCY EKLUND LATER, LINDA LEE, KATHARINE MYERS,
LAUREN NELSON PACKARD, SCOTT TENNENT, PAUL WAGNER, JOSEPH WESTON,
AND DEB WOOD OF PRINCETON ARCHITECTURAL PRESS —KEVIN C. LIPPERT,
PUBLISHER.

LIBRARY OF CONGRESS CATALOG-IN-PUBLICATION DATA
PERRY, MICHAEL, 1981 JULY 19-
HAND JOB: A CATALOG OF TYPE / MICHAEL PERRY.
254 P. : CHIEFLY ILL. (SOME COL.); 26 CM.
ISBN 978-1-56898-626-5 (ALK PAPER)
1. TYPE AND TYPE-FOUNDING--SPECIMENS. 2. TYPE DESIGNERS.
3. TYPOGRAPHERS. 4. PRINTING—HISTORY—20TH CENTURY. I. TITLES
Z 250.A2P46 2007
686.2'2—dc22

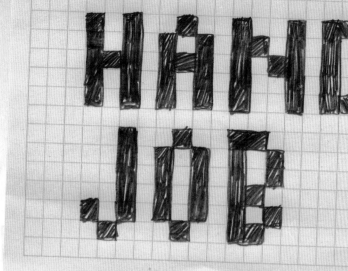

HAND JOB

DEDICATED TO MY
FATHER AND GRANDMOTHER!

SPECIAL THANKS TO: MOM, JIM GENTRY, GRANDPA,
ANNA WOLF, DAN KEENAN, DAMIEN CORRELL,
JIM DATZ, AND EVERYONE ELSE WHO HELPED
THIS BECOME REAL. ♡

THE ~~LIFE~~
THE LIFE
THE FOOD
THE WORK
THE ENTERTAINMENT
THE FUCKERS

THIS BOOK IS TYPE SET IN:

BRYANT
BY ERIC OLSON
www.processtypefoundry

ABCDEFGHIJKLMNOPQRSTUVWXYZ
abcdefghijklmnopqrstuvwxyz
1234567890

HUSSY
BY DAMIEN CORRELL
www.damiencorrell.com

ABCDEFGHIJKLMNOPQRSTUVWXYZ
ABCDEFGHIJKLMNOPQRSTUVWXYZ
1234567890

TABLE OF CONTENTS

PRE FACE

By Michael Perry

Hand Job came about on something of a whim. While filling sketchbooks and doodling away on random sheets of paper for years, contemplating Post-its with illustrated type, like little poems, in front of my computer, it never once occurred to me that a book about hand typography could be something the world needed. The initial idea began as a desire to see all of the work that I love together in one place. It has since turned into a curatorial celebration of the hand typography of my peers. This book is for everyone who has the ability to transform words into art.

Hand type may not always be the right answer or the most time-effective solution, but it is definitely the most fun. It's the answer I go to most often. It shapes my work and the work of so many around me. It is the answer that keeps the artist from taking himself or herself too seriously and infuses some fun into an industry that sometimes takes itself too seriously. It reveals the hand of the maker, and its viewer finds comfort in that: the artist illustrated by lines made crooked from too many cups of coffee.

I don't claim to know what the future holds for hand typography, nor have I attempted here to convey a history of its evolution. I simply want to show what hand type is today and what it means to me—to leave a mark of its impact on art.

The solutions enclosed in this book are full of magic; each page is its own, wholly shaped by the artist's unique process, each a study of carefully executed composition, of accident, line, obsession, color, and craft. The artists are indexed alphabetically, each behind detailed letters created by Luke Ramsey and A.J. Purdy. You'll also find photographs—photos of artist's studios, of type I've found out in the world, of the places and tools that help make typography come to life. My hope is that the work on these pages will open a window into the soul of typography and hold strong to the shining moments where other typography books leave off.

Making this book has been amazing. I knew what I wanted it to look like the minute I sat down to work on it—page after page of color and excitement. Every artist's submission was so different from the others', and receiving each was like opening a wonderful gift. Thank you to everyone who has made this book even more remarkable than I hoped it would be.

Some observations on the act of working by hand.

Commonly, an essay, attempting to sum up the subject matter, occupies this space. The expected route is to give an overview of the field at hand and then map the dominant strands of style, working methods, etc. There is no shortage of these editorials in the design press; many have run the party line: of "Handmade type is expressive and therefore may be very fitting for some of your clients' needs." So, lets skip that. What follows is a collection, developed in the last twelve years, of observations of and insights into making things with typewriters, markers, Letraset, photocopiers, glue sticks, Adobe Streamline, and the occasional chicken wire.

I'm betting (not a lot, mind you—like a ten-spot or something) that most of the people in this book work by hand because they want to, not because it's the "appropriate solution to the design problem at hand." I've come up with some pretty good lines to justify, for example, why the type was copied from a going-out-of-business-sale sign or a meatpacking ad. Now, at different times I've had different levels of conceptual anal-retentiveness, and I might have needed to do some philosophical B.S.-ing just to get myself to do the work. But one does what one must to make things happen, and I'd rather live with a flyer bearing some bizarre type I pulled from a sign that no longer exists than one I set in some typeface that I'm not even sure I liked but "fit the concept." If you need some inspiration to go out on your own, just get a job where it's never appropriate to use hand-drawn stuff. You'll be poor and happy working in your living room in no time at all.

I feel a bit more alive when I'm working the type with my hands; today's logic says I'm being totally inefficient, maybe even painfully slow, but I get to reflect on the subject in the same way a painter does. The work is happening letter by letter and taking shape, and I have to ask, "Is this really working, or am I wasting a whole bunch of time?"

It's the difference between you and the cubicle guys, right? You want to prove that you can get something done without sitting in front of a screen. Not even prove…it's more like I don't want to be that guy living in front of the computer screen. Now I'll contradict myself by saying that the computer makes it incredibly easy for designers to be totally process-driven when working by hand, knowing that they can use the computer to edit and assemble. A lot of the designers I know employ the following working method: they build a bunch of source material through drawing, photocopies, or whatever, creating page after page of the words they might need, but then hold off on judgment until it's all scanned.

It's a pretty great feeling when you've spent five hours at a light table, burning through .005 Pigma Micron pens, and you can tell your boss is like, "I am not paying this dude

to trace." But the people in charge always seem to appreciate it when the printed piece comes through and looks nothing like the other stuff on the market.

I can't always get to where I'm going by doing things the way they're supposed to be done. This isn't a rant against the computer or the "rules" or whatever; it's simply that "if you change the process, you change the product" (thank you, Elliot Earls, for that quote). I trust that a kernel of an idea will turn into something greater than its beginning. It's not as if this is a digital-age concern; these ways of working with the sketchbook and Letraset and photocopies and stencils and whatever else I can get my hands on were just as valid in 1965 or 1925. (Think of that Dada poster by Kurt Schwitters and Theo Van Doesburg and remember that both of those guys made at least some cash by being regular graphic designers who set type. They practically invented modern typography.) Let the baseline drift and wobble, and let the viewer know that a person made this. Try your best. Don't fuck around. It can't be perfect, which is so much the beauty of it.

Every time I put a mark down with my hands, I intuitively learn something: a wrong angle, bad spacing, an ugly r, or "That one's hot, let's not fuck it up" (and then you do anyway: restraint is for suckers). Start at zero and add; everything is a decision to be made. When working on the computer, I get a pasteboard full of stuff, and then a lot of the work can be done in one big gesture—bang, four paragraphs of copy down, punctuation is hung, and the font tells Illustrator what to do with the leading and spacing and kerning. Yes, there's intuition as I feel my way through the layout, but the decision-making is macro—What typeface? What size? Should I adjust the leading? What are the proportions? When drawing a word with a pen, I work on a micro scale, and decisions are made on every matter: How am I going to space this? Do I care about the baseline? Is it even the same typestyle? Why can't I draw today? All defaults are gone. It's me versus the world; even when I lose, at least it's an interesting place to be.

Two.

The story of modernism (of painting or whatever) goes something like this: new technology (photography) comes along and frees old technology (painting) from its previous obligations to standards, perfection, representation, or what-have-you, and modern painting is created. Once upon a time, graphic designers would've been expected to have a decent number of lettering skills even if it were just to work up an initial layout. Then the computer completely removed the need for those skills. By rendering hand lettering obsolete, the computer strips it of its previous obligations and imbues the very act of lettering with a level of meaning that it has not had. Now I use my hands because I want mistakes, quirks, and imperfections—those qualities that give my work warmth. Keep in mind that, at different times in history, that warmth could've gotten you fired. Now we view these results as the elemental quality of working by hand.

Scott Makela once said that he wouldn't sell any more of his typefaces, because he wanted to "protect his DNA." I've always liked the idea that our handwriting and lettering—the shape, the spacing, the quality—is our DNA and is unique to our work.

Three.

I've never had much luck using a photo of some great, oddly spaced hand-painted sign and attempting to replicate it with a computer. Maybe I just haven't tried hard enough. I don't know if mistake-induced spacing is all that interesting; it's more the full package of aesthetics, quirks, and ideas that I am after. When I find a two-word sign with a randomly italicized I, it is going to be just that in a line of Helvetica. But when I try to draw a typeface based off that sign, then that I becomes an integral element. This more or less overlooks one of my own motivations for copying type from signs and photos anyway: to pay homage to the people whose handiwork is all around me yet rarely considered.

Four.

A sense of history is embedded in this kind of work, even if it's only at a glance. When using the same tools as those who came before me, I'm going to cop some moves. I think there's a certain retro quality to a lot of this work, which makes sense. If I'm using the same tools as a sign painter from the 1920s, a 1970s illustrator, or the graffiti writer down the block, it makes more sense to look at their work than that of some dude who's setting allcaps Helvetica Neue. I would go so far as to say that a lot of people working by hand are directly inspired by seeing work done by others using the same medium and believing in it.

Photo by: Anna Wolf

ABCDEF
GHIJKL
MNOPQ
RSTUVW
XYZ.,;:!?
1234567
890

emily CM anderson
www.ecmanderson.net

Emily C. M. Anderson is a graphic designer
who loves hot-pink and metallic inks, paper,
screen printing, sewing, pink champagne,
formats, hi Liters, and cupcakes. Currently a
resident of the West Coast, transplanted from
the Midwest, Emily studied at the Minneapolis
College of Art and Design and at the Acad-
emie voor beeldende kunst en vormgeving
Arnhem, in the Netherlands.

www.TYLERASKEW.com

Tyler Askew is a New York–based graphic designer
and art director with a passion for typography. His
diverse portfolio includes branding, packaging,
editorial, and type development for clients in the
music, fashion, advertising, and nonprofit worlds.
While studying communication design at the
Atlanta College of Art, Tyler traveled to London,
where he worked under typographer and
designer Ian "Swifty" Swift. For more than ten
years, Tyler has nurtured a loyal private client
base that includes MAC, Oscar de la Renta,
Equinox Fitness, David Yurman, and Bill Blass.
Since 1999, Tyler has been a consultant and
writer for Straight No Chaser and has deejayed
internationally.

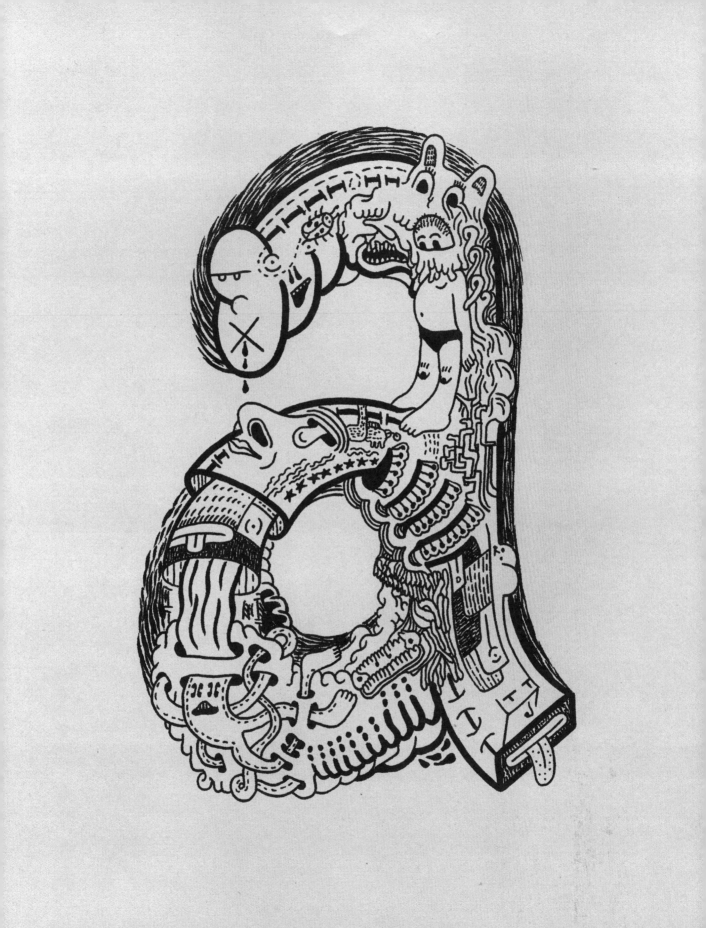

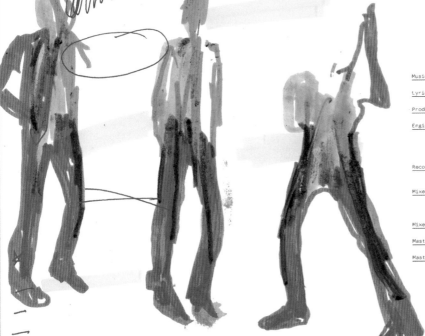

Melodious Owl, 2005
Album art
Offset printing

Chariots, 2004
Album-release poster
Silk screen

Strand

ABCDEFGHIJKLMN
OPQRSTUVWXYZ

abcdefghjiklmn
opqrstuvwxyz

0123456789 @&& :;..

Strand, 2004
Typeface and poster
Hair and offset printing

Evergrowing elements woven together to make an intricate whole.

Strand

inkdup.

ABCDEFG
HiJKLMNO
PQRSTUV
WXYZ.

Inkdup, 2000
Typeface
Ink

ANDY BEACH b. 1976

Andy Beach, born in 1976, lives and works in Philadelphia. As a father, husband, homeowner, designer, collector, builder, renovator, and man of letters, he's got a lot on his mind. He spends his days as a graphic designer at Urban Outfitters.

Kate Bingaman

OBSESSIVECONSUMPTION.COM

Kate Bingaman has always been in love with her handwriting. She first flexed her typographic muscles by forging her friends' parents' signatures on elementary school band practice sheets. She never forged her parents' signatures because she actually liked to practice her flute. At some point she veered away from a budding career in forgery and now uses her powers for good. Obsessiveconsumption.com is Kate's baby, and she is constantly drawing the dumb things that she buys (and words that describe the dumb things that she buys). She is an assistant professor of graphic design at Mississippi State University. Typography is her favorite class to teach.

daniel black

allthosetwos.com

Dan Black was born in Galveston, Texas, in 1978 and hasn't been back since. He graduated from the Minneapolis College of Art and Design in 2003 and is currently working at the 2222 Screenprint Facility in Minneapolis, designing and printing posters, record sleeves, and other things.

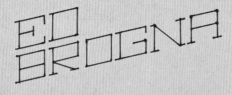

ED BROGNA

Ed Brogna lives and works in Philadelphia. He studied painting at the School of the Museum of Fine Arts Boston and at Tufts University. He enjoys spending weekends with his wife, Stephanie, and son, Harry, and surf fishing off the South Jersey shore.

hellosoandsew.com

Barbara Botting was once a clothing designer for Urban Outfitters and Gap before returning to her primary objective: making lovely things. To that end, she and Jenn Cote formed SoAndSew, an independent label of one-off clothing and accessories. In addition to maintaining her day job as an apparel and still-life stylist, she is developing a new body of fashion-based work about her experiences in the rag trade and her love of industrial materials.

RICH BROWD

RICHBROWD.COM
DEADKIDZ.COM

Rich Browd is twenty-four years old and lives in Chinatown in New York City. He works as a designer for MTV. When not at work, Rich enjoys making music videos. He falls in and out of love almost every day.

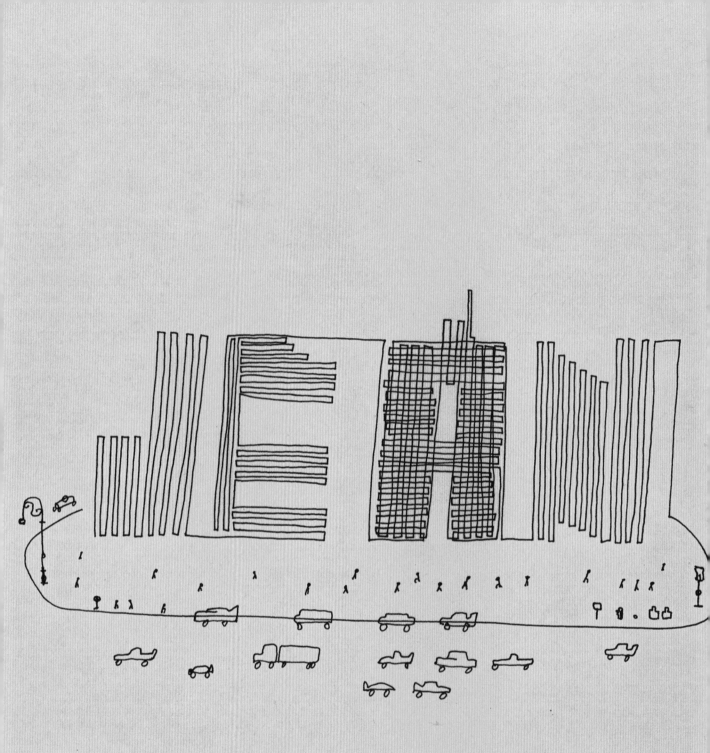

All Kinds of People, 2005–06
Miscellaneous type
Pen

CAN I GET A...

PEAS ON EARTH

Engulf & Devour

HITTING SWITCHES

LEG MAN

"THE GENTLE TOUCH"

Yoshitomo Nara: Nothing Ever Happ

You always lose on 'Ego'

BIG SHINY BLADES

HAND MADE

Love Your Money!, 2006
Posters, wallpaper, and
Drawings
Digital prints

MBNA Credit Card Statement,
2005
Hand-drawn credit-card statement
Pen and ink on bristol board

Apple Credit Account

MBNA
At Your Service
www.mbnanetaccess.com

PAYMENT DUE	NEW BALANCE
08/21/05	$2,028.36
Total Min DUE	Amount enclosed
$43.00	

Detach top Portion & Return w/ Payment

make check payable to: MBNA AMERICA
P.O. BOX 15289
WILMINGTON, DE 19886-5289

FOR account information call 1.888.637.6262
Print change of address or new telephone number

Address _____

city _____ State ____ Zip ____

(.   ) _____ (.   ) _____
HOME phone   WORK phone

KATE BINGAMAN
PO BOX 455
MS STATE UNIV   MS 39762-045555

credit line	cash or credit Available	pays in billing cycle	closing Date	total Min payment Due	payment Due Date
$2,400.00	$371.64	30	07/21/05	$43.00	08/21/05

POSTING Date	TRANS Date	Ref #	Category	transactions JULY 2005 Statement	charges	credits (CR)

Payments & Credits

07/15   PAYMENT - NET ACCESS   44.00 CR

TOTAL FOR BILLING CYCLE FROM 06/22/2005 THROUGH 07/2/2005 $0.00
$44.00 CR

IMPORTANT NEWS

Pay your Bill Quickly with the pay-by-phone service. Call 1-866-297-9258 to use this automated service. Payments post the same or next business day. Plan ahead FOR Life's ups & Downs PROTECT your MBNA CREDIT RATING today! Call 1.800.280.8942, or visit WWW.MBNAPROTECT.com. visit WWW.MBNANETACCESS.com — your online source FOR statements, Payments, & more!

SUMMARY OF TRANSACTIONS

Previous Balance	(-) Payment & credits	(+) Advances	(+) other charges	(+) Periodic Rate FINANCE charges	(+) Transaction Fee FINANCE charges	(=) New Balance Total
$2,043.77	$44.00	$0.00	$0.00	$28.59	$0.00	$2,028.36

TOTAL MINIMUM PAYMENT DUE

Past Due Amount 0.00
Current Payment 43.00
Total MIN Payment
Due 43.00

FINANCE CHARGE SCHEDULE

	Periodic Rate	Corresponding ANNUAL % Rate	Balance subject to Finance charge
A. ADVANCES	0.046547% DLY*	16.99%	$1,993.35
B. ADVANCES	0.046547% DLY*	16.99%	$0.00
C. OTHER CHARGES	0.046547% DLY*	16.99%	$53.99

For This Billing Period:
ANNUAL PERCENTAGE RATE 16.99%

Obsessive Consumption Studio,
2006
Thermo-Fax screens, handmade
pillows, wallpaper, couch*
*Couch shown was the first object
ever documented by Obsessive
Consumption.

Make Believe, 2005
Album-announcement postcard
Five-color screen print on French
cover stock

Series 2+3, 2004
Poster illustration
Four-color screen print on French
cover stock

Call for submissions, 2005
Poster for Minnesota Film Arts
One-color screen print on French
cover stock

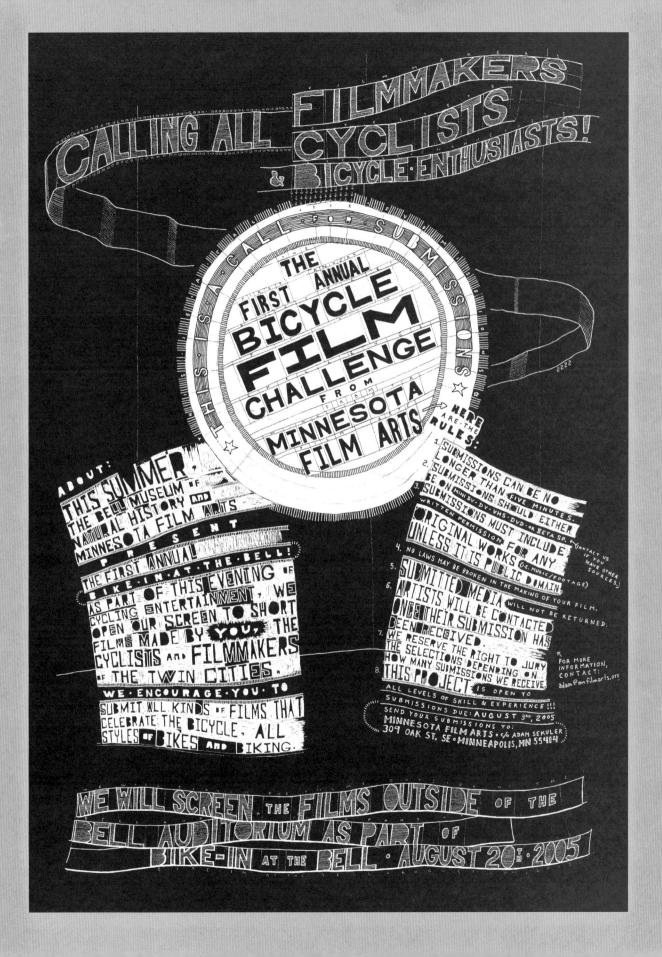

Thank You, 2004
Urban Outfitters Thanks You card
Four-color offset printing

Preservation, 2002
Institute of Contemporary Art,
Space 1026
Letraset on paper

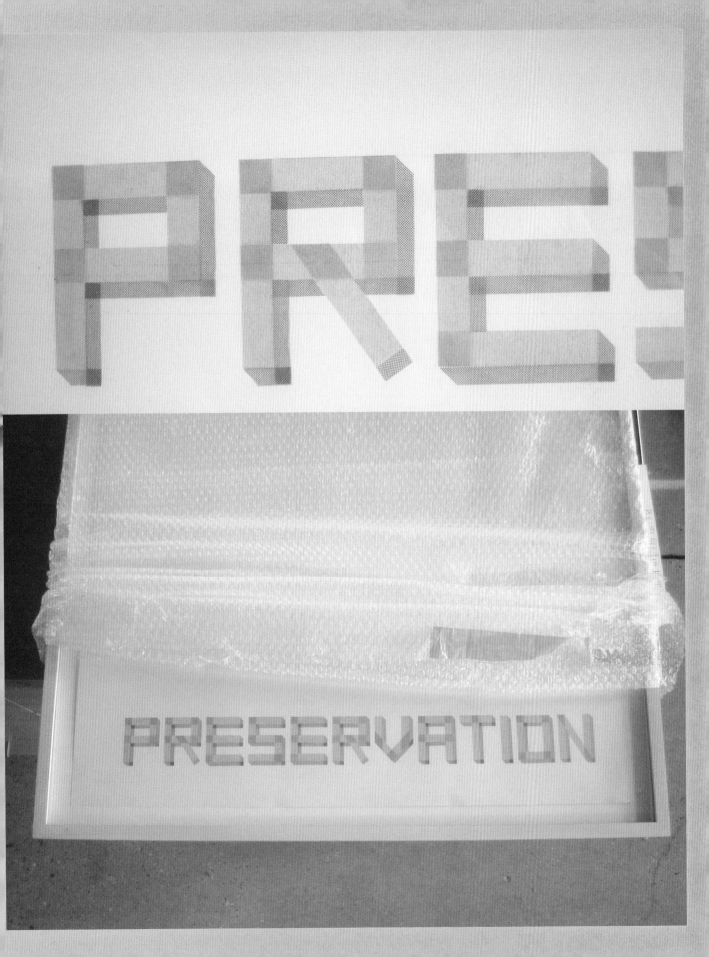

Untitled, 2005
Sketches
Pen and miscellaneous paper

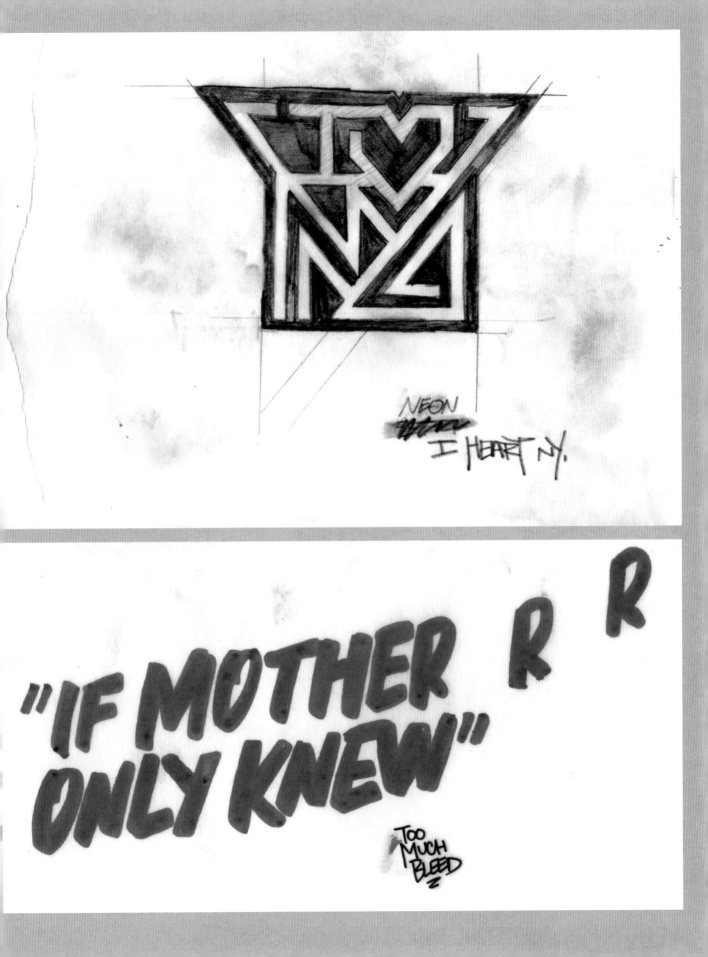

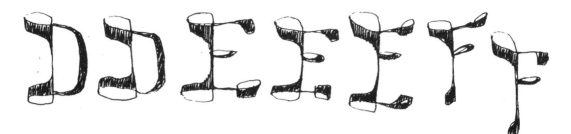

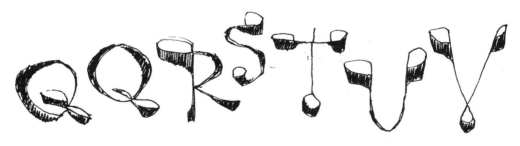

Untitled, 2005
Sketch
Pen on paper

José Ricardo Cabral Cabaco was born in Maputo, Mozambique, in 1965. He graduated in industrial design from the Institute of Visual Arts, Design, and Marketing (IADE) in Portugal and has worked as an industrial designer in the glass, ceramics, furniture, and automotive industries. he has also done some gigs in fashion. José currently works for Wieden+Kennedy as a Nike creative director for the Latin American region. José will always work as a graphic designer. He has kept a journal since the age of ten.

Robin Cameron is Rocamm and was born in 1981 in the interior of British Columbia. She graduated from Emily Carr Institute of Art and Design (ECIAD) in 2004 and lives in Brooklyn, New York. Her work has been shown in Vancouver, Toronto, Seattle, Chicago, and Tokyo and has appeared in *Arkitip*, *Adbusters*, *Made*, and *Nieves Books*. Primarily a typographer and illustrator, Robin has an affinity for hand-touched graphics.

Deanne Cheuk
www.deannecheuk.com

Deanne Cheuk was recognized as one of Print magazine's "20 under 30" and as one of Time magazine's "best people of 2004." She is a contributor to Vogue Nippon, America, Dazed and Confused, Nylon, BlackBook, Flaunt, and the magazine. She has art-directed and designed numerous magazines, including Big and Tokion, and has been commissioned by such companies as Nike, Converse, Sprint, ESPN, and MTV2. She is renowned for her graphic zine, Neomu. In 2005, she released her first book, Mushroom Girls Virus. She is one of three partners in the clothing line Liness.

Paul Clark was born and raised in Pittsburgh, Pennsylvania, and currently resides in Brooklyn, New York. He has been lucky enough to see his work appear in books and magazines and on television. His art has been seen both domestically and abroad in a number of gallery shows. Currently, Paul enjoys the company of his girlfriend and baby boy and vows to skateboard and make art every day.

HTTP://WWW.DAMIENCORRELL.com

Damien Correll is twenty-four years old and has been drawing letters forever. In middle school, he and his friends would draw comics, but because he was such a shit illustrator, he did all of the titling. Per the recommendation of his sixth-grade art teacher, Damien took out a bunch of books on graphic design. That summer, he relabeled everything he owned with traced letters out of calligraphy books. He had three favorite typefaces at that time, two of which made it onto his first business card, printed at the local mall. Damien even took an unsolicited stab at redesigning his middle school's logo in MS Paint. Despite all that, it was having every girl at school request bubble letters on her folders and notebooks that sealed his fate as a designer.

"EVERYONE IS A MOON AND HAS A DARK SIDE WICH THEY NEVER SHOW TO ANYBODY."
MARK TWAIN

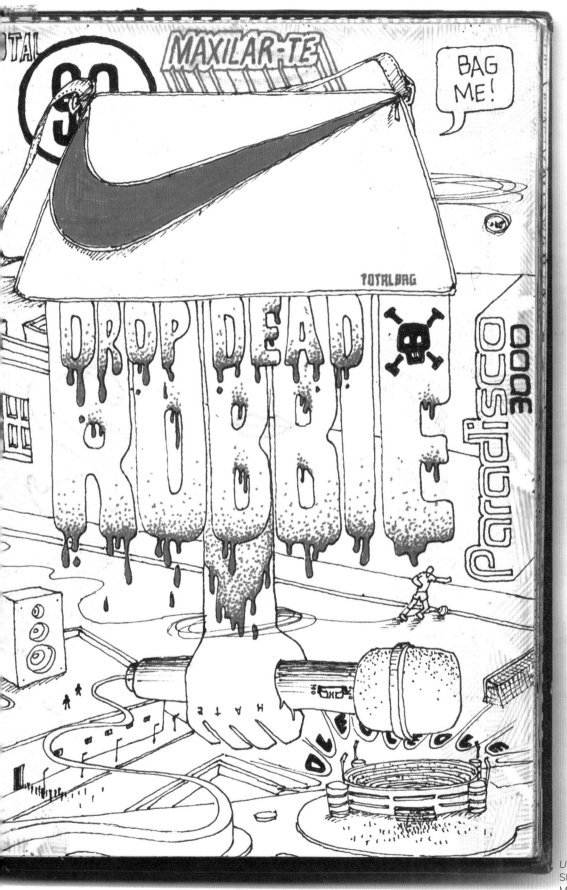

Untitled, 2000–2006
Sketchbook sketches
Mixed media

Untitled, 2000–2006
Sketchbook sketches
Mixed media

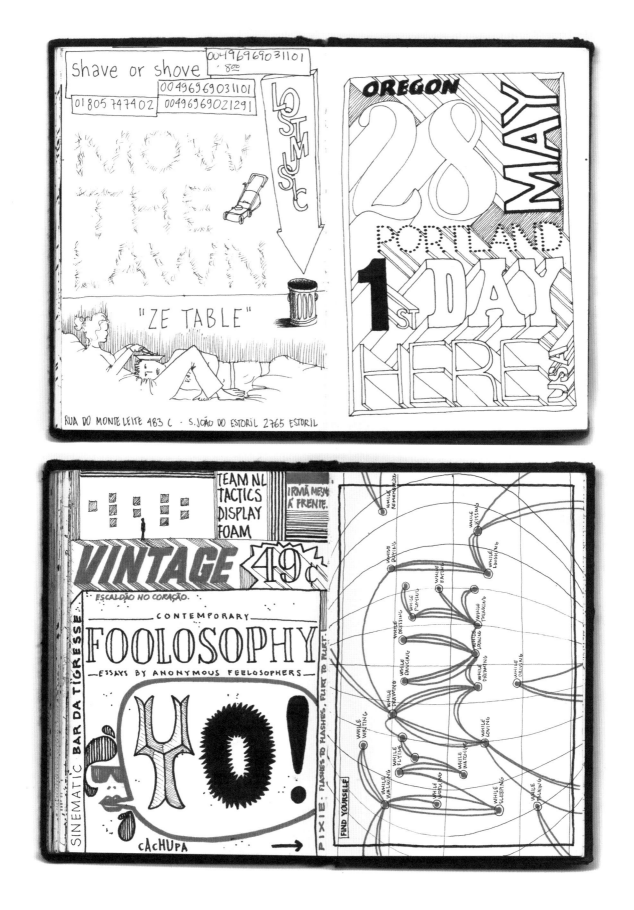

*Cleanliness is Next to
Godliness*, 2004
Illustration for Notions
of the Faux Naive
Photograph; silk screen on cloth

Dry Hump, 2005
Illustration for Illustrators
Union Almanac
Silk screen; brush and ink

Blob Typeface, 2005
Experimental typeface
Pen on paper

Various Flyers, 2004–05
Flyers for various events
in Vancouver
Variable processes

King of Art, 2005
Tokion magazine, March/April
2005 issue
Watercolor

Various King of Titles, 2004
Tokion magazine, September/
October 2004 issue
Watercolor

KING OF SCENE

KING OF ART

KING OF BRAND

KING OF DESIGN

KING OF FASHION

Michel Gondry

Michel Gondry and Takeshi Kitano
Titles, 2005
Tokion magazine, March/April
2005 issue
Watercolor

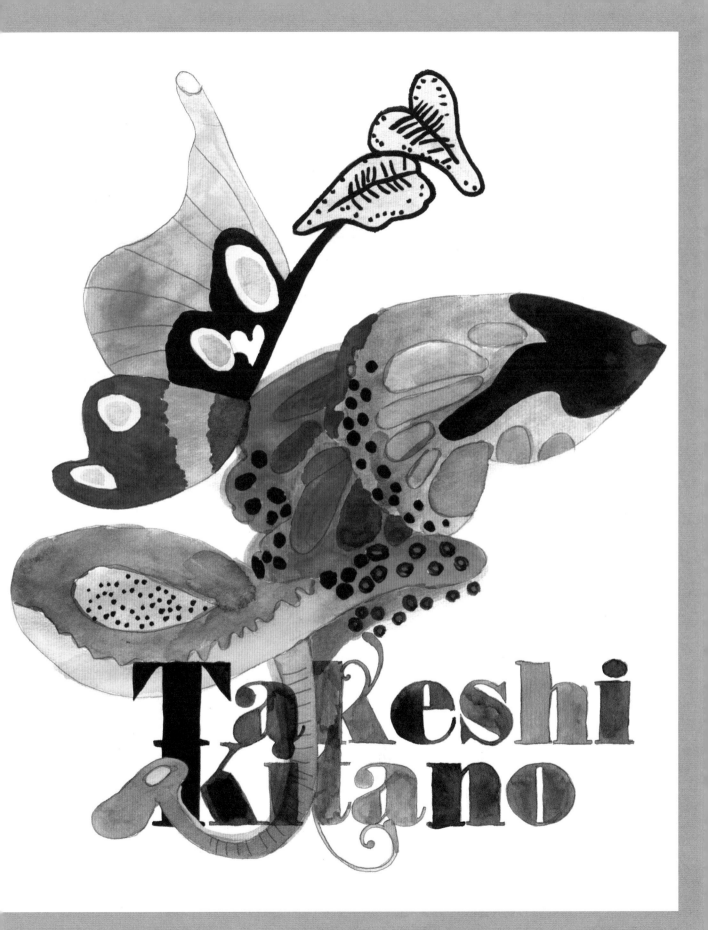

Three Typefaces, 2005
Pen on paper

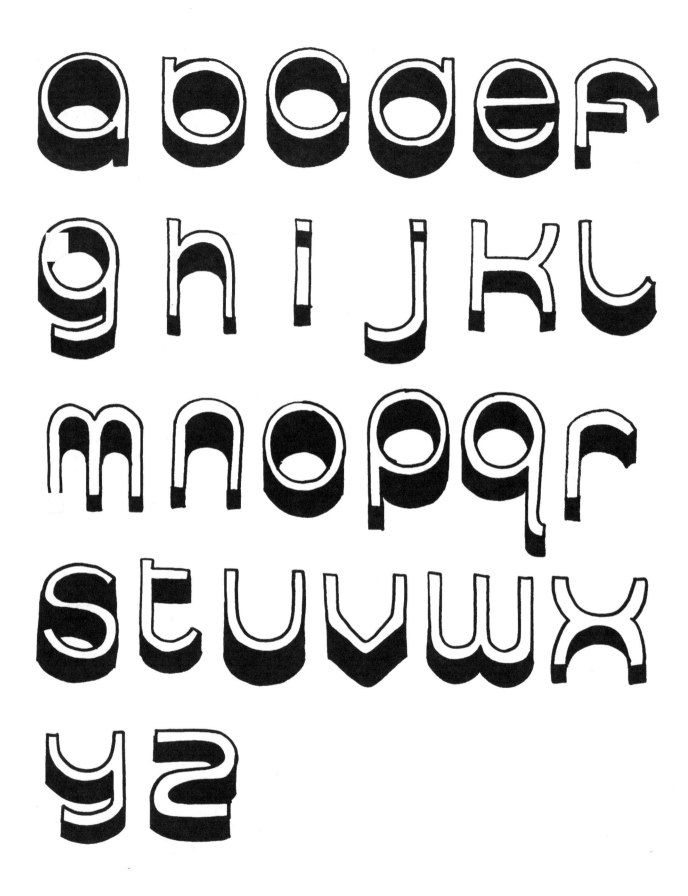

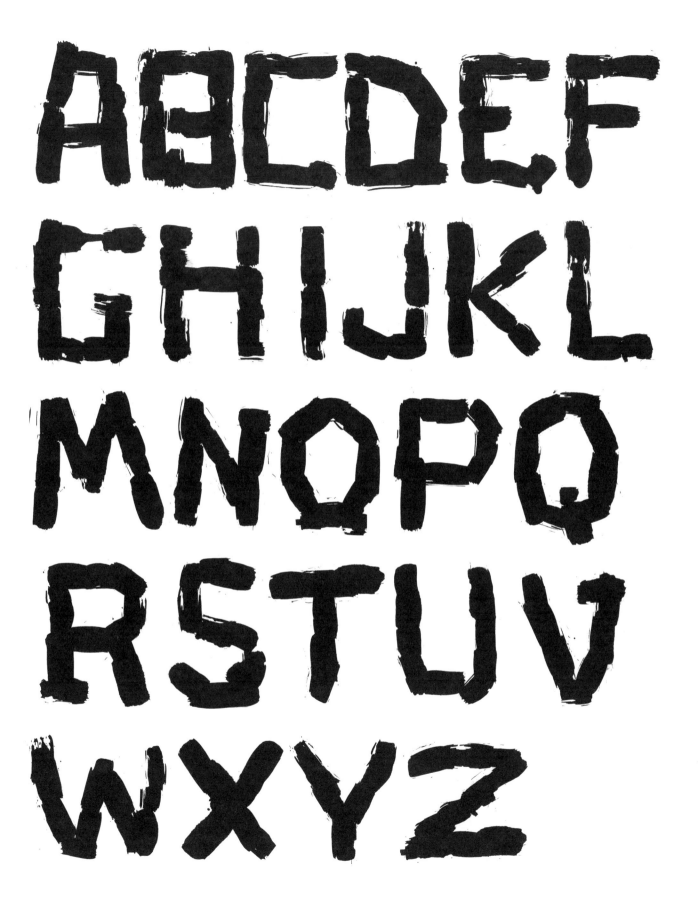

Hugs for You, 2005
Log type
Pen on paper

Eldarondo, 2006
Swindle magazine, Issue 6
Pen on paper

SUNDAY
MONDAY
TUESDAY
WEDNESDAY
THURSDAY
FRIDAY
SATURDAY

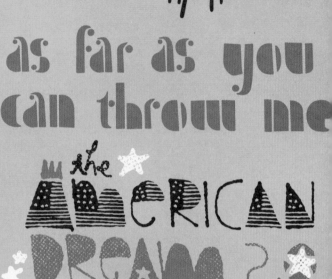

Smile

as far as you
can throw me

the AMERICAN
DREAM 2.0

MOSS ST.
SPRUCE ST.
BLUEJAY DR.
SHEAFF LN.
PINE ST.
JFK BLD.
20TH ST.
WINSTON DR.
3RD ST.
11TH ST.

ROME
rome
Rome
ROME ROME
RQME ROME
rome
ROME
rome

Misc-type, 2006
Rome SDS, *Swindle* magazine,
Issue 7
Miscellaneous type, Pen on paper

Rec Room, 2006
Playgroup
Wood Blocks

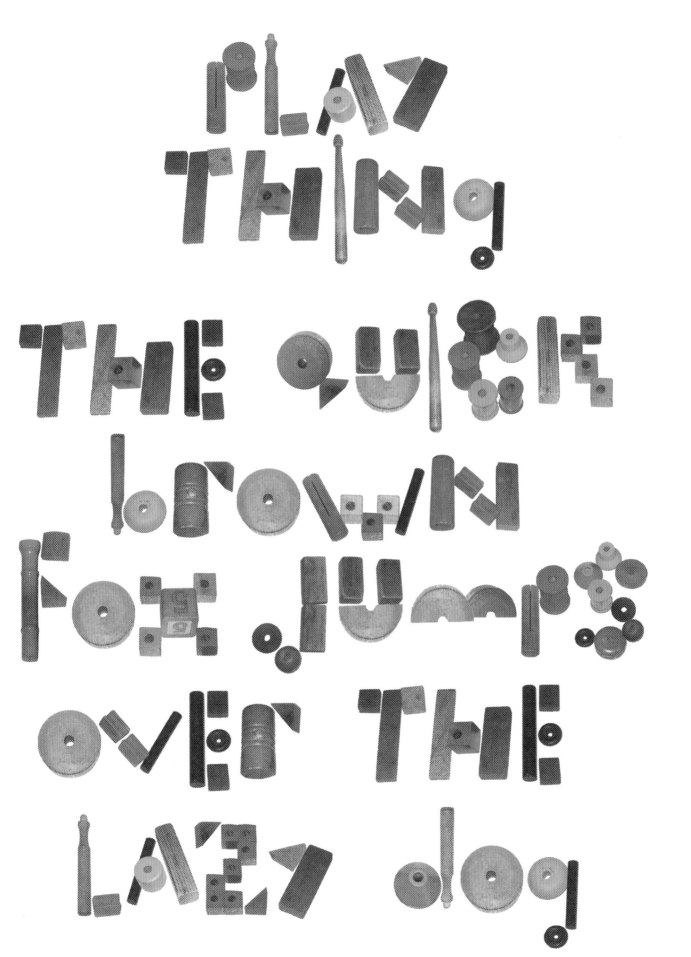

JEREMY DEAN

WWW. COMFORTABLE LEAD.
BLOGSPOT. COM.

Jeremy Dean was raised on punk, skateboard-
ing, and zines. He received his design education at Temple's Tyler School of Art, shunning
the computer in favor of tape, scissors, photocopies, and press type. From these scraps
came a font called Crackhouse, which Jeremy
designed to use on school projects to annoy
his type teachers. Crackhouse found a home at
House Industries and eventually secured him
a type-designer position with unlimited copier
privileges. Drawing from his years of experi-
ence with House Industries and later Urban
Outfitters, he founded Comfortable Lead in late
2003. Jeremy has now reunited with former
House Industries homeboys and ex–Zoltar the
Magnificent prankster, Barnzley, to form the
clothing brand House33.

DEMO-DESIGN.COM

In 1997 Justin Fines founded Demo. Born
out of the love of his hometown, Detroit, and
its music, Demo got its start by churning out
flyers and ephemera for the city's then-thriving
electronic music scene. Nine years, three cities,
and countless projects later, Fines has found a
home for Demo in New York City. In his work,
the golden tint of nostalgia for a suburban
childhood blends with the hulking abandoned
factories and mansions of the Motor City.
This combination creates a graphic language
that balances between hope and cynicism.
Fines's work has been featured in publications
worldwide; recent projects include a toy for
Superdeux & RedMagic, a Hong Kong company; an artist-series board for Zoo York; and
a series of designs for the Truth Campaign.

House 33 and Destroy, 2004
House 33 poster
Two-color screen print

Misc-type, 2002–05
Self-generated type
Pen on paper

Untitled, 2005
Lumpen magazine Issue 95,
Two-color offset printing

Untitled, 2004
Shirt design for 2K by Gingham,
based on an image from Battlezine
with Struggle Inc., 2004
Pen on paper

CURTIS FLANAGAN

curtisFlanagan.com

Curtis Flanagan lives and goes to school in Philadelphia. When not designing, he enjoys making things such as grandma's apple pie. He also enjoys handmade books and exploring various printing methods. Growing up in Iowa, he spent much of his time drawing fantastic mind scapes in his sketchbooks and dreaming of faraway places.

www.DanFunderburgh.com

Dan Funderburgh was reared in the Midwest in the 1980s. The son of two biologists, Dan attended a well-meaning state university and soon after left for the champagne dreams of New York City. He co-founded the Thought-Ninjas of North America in 2005 and currently provides art direction and sundry graphics for the skate and apparel industries. Equally attracted to the modern and the baroque, to content and decoration, Dan makes wallpapers, prints, typography, and illustration for select clientele and galleries. He plans on doing this until he figures out a better method of changing the way things are.

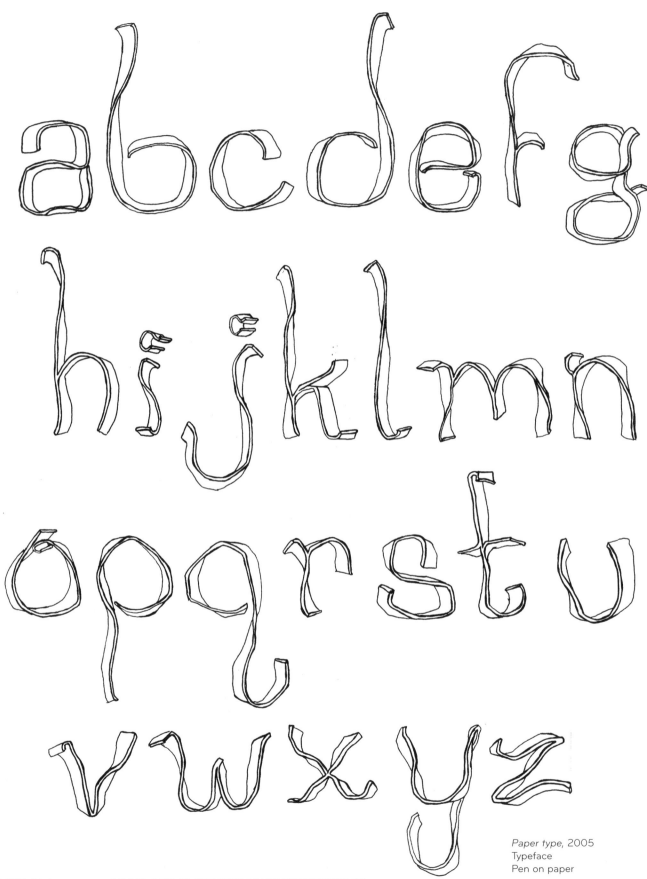

Paper type, 2005
Typeface
Pen on paper

Alphabet, 2006
Typeface
Pen on paper

Random Type Doodles, 2004
Pen on paper

WE DON'T KNOW COOL PEOPLE

why is this?

We Don't Know Cool People, 2005
Personal mantra
Pen on paper

WWW.THEPRESSURE.ARG

Adam Garcia is currently a student at the
Minneapolis College of Art and Design. He is
an Aries and is addicted to sugar. When not
creating album covers for his part-time job at a
CD-manufacturing company, he does freelance
work in design and illustration, makes music
under the name Snakebird, and in general
does the best he can to support the art and
music community in the Twin Cities.

WWW.GLUEKIT.COM

Working under the moniker of Gluekit,
Christopher Sleboda is a graphic designer and
illustrator. "Glue is good," Sleboda says. After
all, glue is that which holds everything together.
For Sleboda, things often get sticky in New
Haven, Connecticut, where he has set up shop.
His illustrations have appeared in *New York*
magazine, the *New York Times, GQ, Esquire,
Spin, Wired, Nylon, How, Print,* and *Step.*

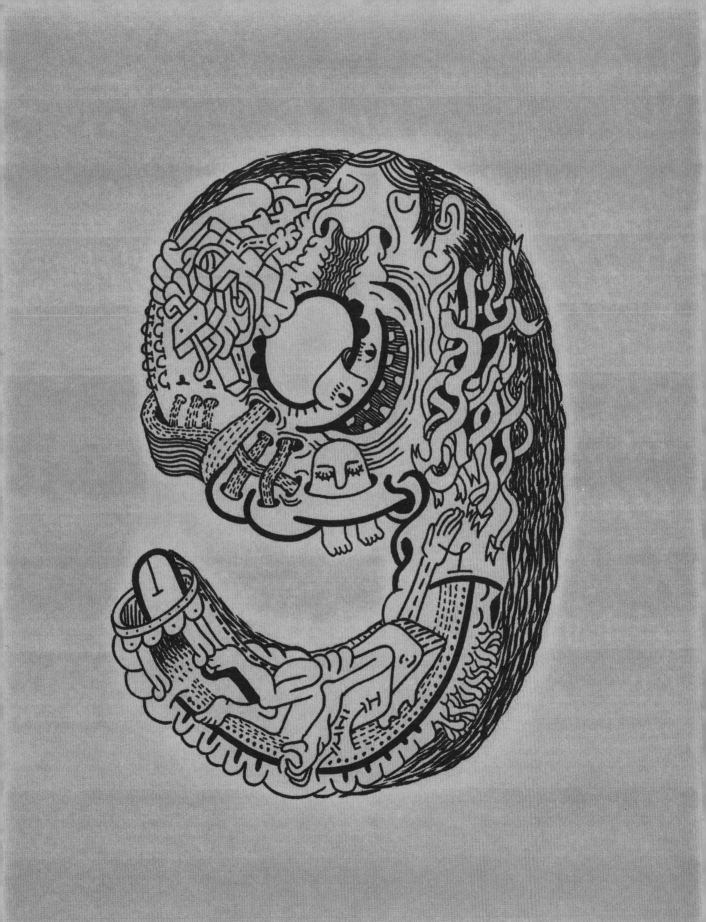

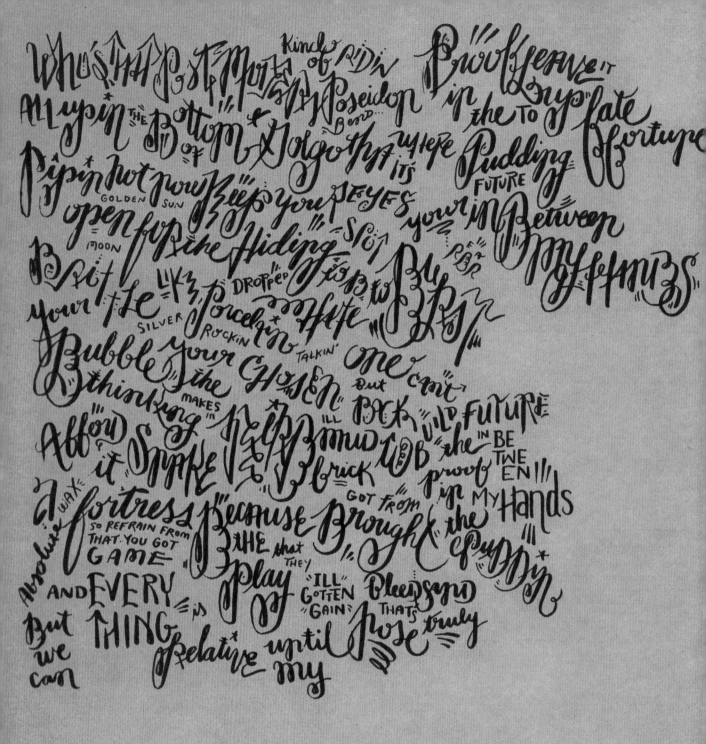

Lyric sheet, 2005
Snakebird lyrics, taken from
sketchbooks
Pen on paper

Untitled, 2005
Faesthetic magazine, issue 5
Digital layering of scanned,
hand typography

Calligraphic title sketches, 2005
Personal Work
Ink

VisionQuest booklet spreads, 2005
In-school work
Xerox on newsprint

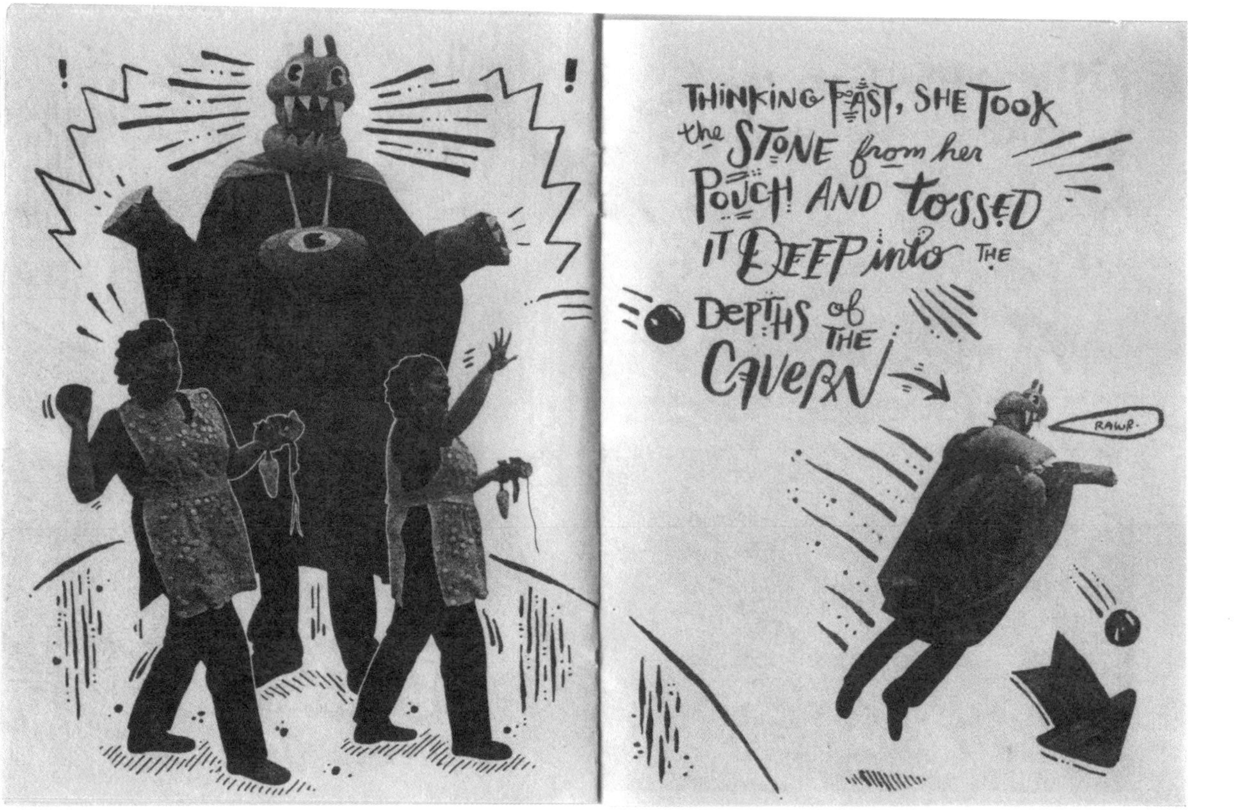
THINKING FAST, SHE TOOK the STONE from her POUCH AND TOSSED IT DEEP into THE DEPTHS of THE CAVERN
RAWR.

AS Mountain Lion INVESTIGATED the NOISE, YOUNG SARA swiftly ESCAPED his LAIR!
RAWR!

Mountain Rocks, 2006
T-shirt for Gluekit
Silk screen, in collaboration with
Amy Jean Porter

I Sing Instruments, 2006
T-shirt for Gluekit
Silk screen

I SING INSTRUM ENTS

GHETTOCROWN.COM
NICHOLAS HANS PASCETTA

Nicholas Hans uses hand type almost every day. He likes the Sanford Uni-ball Onyx pen, with a Fine tip and black ink. Nicholas works for a big company during the day and sometimes does things for friends. He chants Hare Krishna and has a dog named Laxsmi. He is twenty-eight years old, going on seventy-five. His style seems fun, but in fact he's a fun-hating hermit. It cracks him up when he sees his type on a young girl's T-shirt. He wonders if she ever thinks about who designed it. Nicholas is pretty sure she thinks it was a young hip girl and not a grumpy, out-of-the-loop guy with a beard.

m-v-a.com
Sparky Hardisty

Sparky Hardisty was born in Rhode Island in 1977. He started doing graphic design as a teenager, making punk zines. When he realized that he could actually get paid, he promptly enrolled in school, graduating from the Minneapolis College of Art and Design in 2003. He continues to live and work in Minneapolis with his wife, Kim. Designing under the studio name MVA, he works for arts-and-culture clients such as Intermedia Arts.

ADAM HAYES
WWW. MR A HAYES. CO. UK

Adam Hayes is a London–based designer. Hand lettering makes up a large part of his work, for which he utilizes both craft and digital technologies to create typographic designs for his clients, personal projects, and collaborations. Recent works have included commissions for film-title sequences, clothing designs, and television advertisements for companies such as BeamsT, And A, Howies, and Sony.

www. hellochopper.com.

Partners Ethan Trask and Joshua Liberson founded Helicopter in 2002. It has recently received awards from *I.D.* magazine and The Art Directors Club. Based in New York City, its clients include Condé Nast, LTB Media, Capitol Records, and the *New York Times*.

Holly Hopkinson began her career as an illustrator in 2005 while in the midst of studying communication art and design at the Royal College of Art in London. This is the first time she has been published in her short career, but she hopes it won't be the last. Holly's main interest is drawing. Her aim for the future is to become a commercial illustrator and to work in advertising, publishing, and editorial illustration.

Mario Hugo
www. loveworn. com

Mario Hugo is a New York–based artist and designer. He studied fine arts, fell in love with design, left fine arts to study art direction, discovered that "art direction" in education programs is actually another name for "copywriting," and has had a tempestuous affair with illustration ever since. Given his profession (design), Mario spends an inordinate amount of time in front of a computer, but he still feels most honest with a pen and two or more sheets of paper (practice sheets). Mario has worked for MTV, Nike, *W* magazine, 2K by Gingham, and Make Feet Beautiful, among other clients. He has exhibited at various galleries in Barcelona, Brussels, Indonesia, Paris, and New York.

In 2003, Wiebke Schultz, Jan Kruse, and Malte Kaune founded Human Empire in the deep woods of northern Germany. Since April 2006, Human Empire has run its own shop in Hamburg, Germany, where they sell T-shirts, sweatshirts, posters, books, and other things that they design. In addition, the founders of Human Empire sell designs and illustrations and get some money for it. A large part of the work is done for music labels, bands, and musicians. Everyone who means well is welcom— at Human Empire.

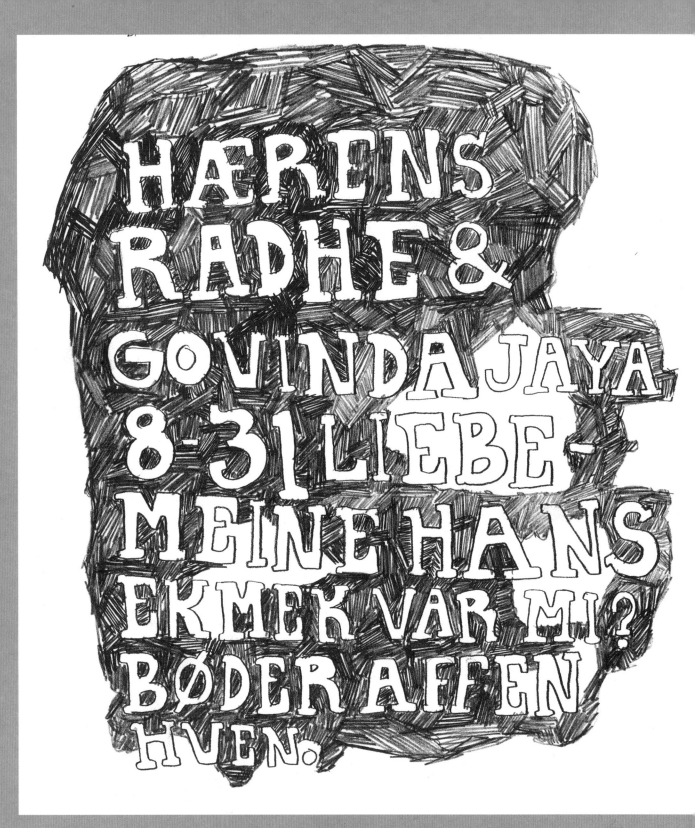

HÆRENS RADHE & GOVINDA JAYA 8-31 LIEBE - MEINE HANS EKMEK VAR MI? BØDER AFFEN HVEN.

Radhe Govinda, 2005
T-Shirt graphic for Urban Outfitters
Pencil on paper

No Toda, 2005
Graphic study for Urban Outfitters
Ink, mixed media, marker

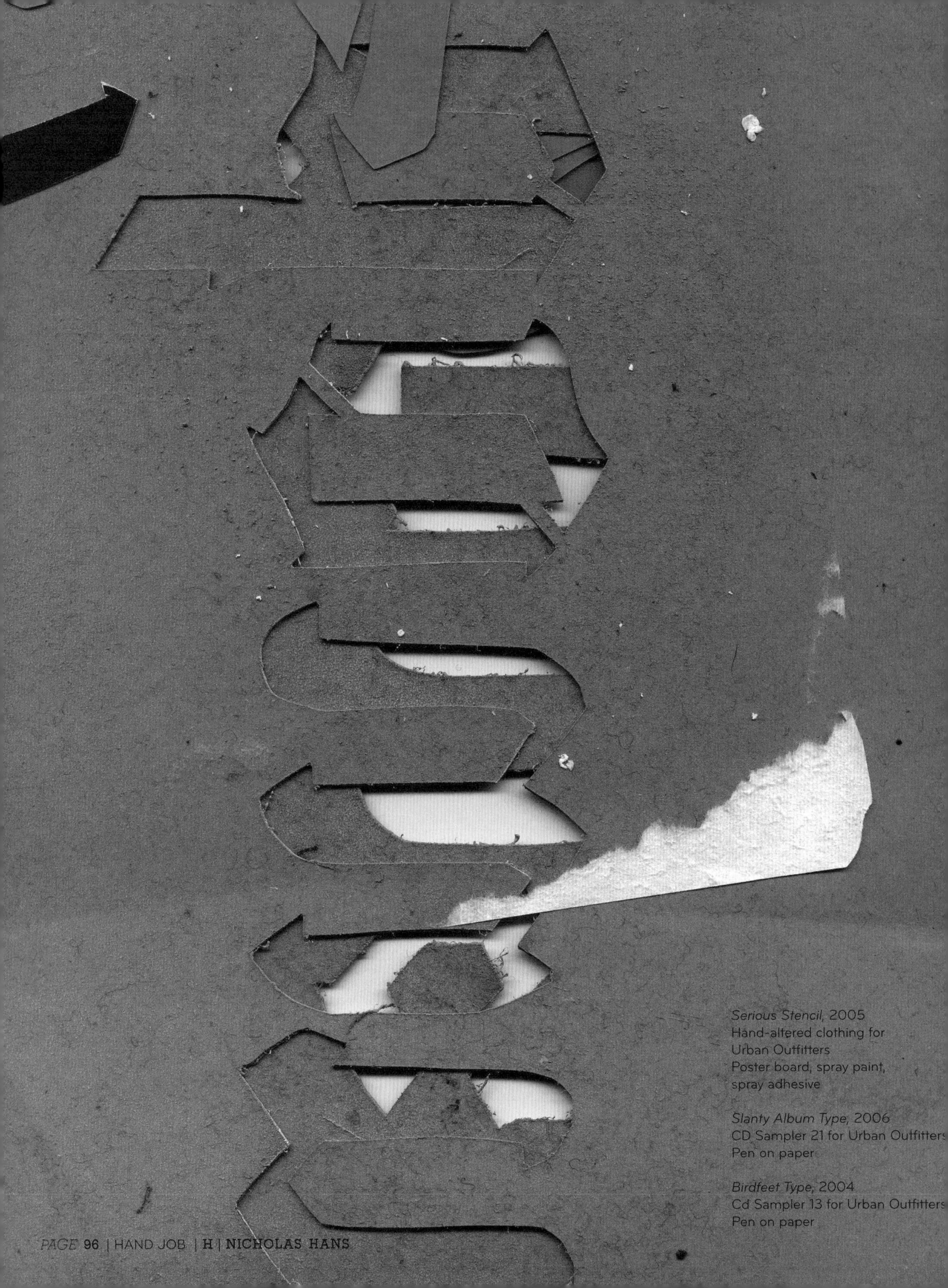

Serious Stencil, 2005
Hand-altered clothing for
Urban Outfitters
Poster board, spray paint,
spray adhesive

Slanty Album Type, 2006
CD Sampler 21 for Urban Outfitters
Pen on paper

Birdfeet Type, 2004
Cd Sampler 13 for Urban Outfitters
Pen on paper

ABCDEF G GHII
JKLMN N OO
P QRS TUVW
X X YZZ

ABCDE FG H I
JKLMNOPQR
S TUVWXY Z
&-1234567890

The Collective: Intensive, 2004
Theater announcement for the
Children's Theatre Company
Two-color offset printing; someone
finally paid me for the use of my
own handwriting

The Encyclopedia of Hip-Hop
Evolution, 2004
Hip-hop flyer for Intermedia Arts
Laserprint, Artists' names hand-
drawn from "For Rent" signs aroun
Minneapolis

Untitled, 2003–04
Type drawn after various photos
of handmade signs from the
designer's personal collection
Pen, marker, and pencil on paper

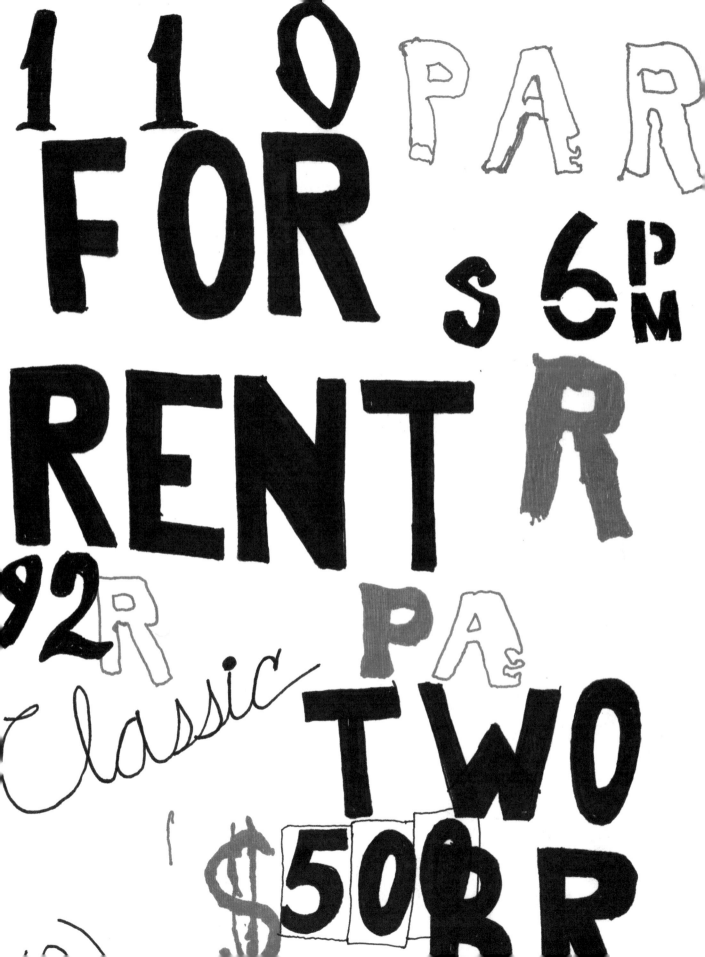

Trunk Road 1, 2005
Scratched photograph. Taken from
a series of works titled *Trunk Road*
Personal Work

ARC 5, 2006
Front cover for the Royal College o
Art magazine, *ARC*.
(www.arcroyal.co.uk)
Line drawing with pen

Hand-drawn Alphabet, 2004
Personal project
Line drawing with pen

BURNING SPEAR

1. OUR MUSIC
2. TRY AGAIN
3. DOWN IN JAMAICA
4. TOGETHER (EXT.MIX)
5. FRIENDS
6. RASTAMAN (EXT.MIX)

GLORY BE
TO JAH ONE
CREATOR.
FOR JAH
SAFETY
FOR JAH
PROVIDENCE
FOR
JAH
GUIDANCE,
AND
PROTECTION.
TOGETHER
WE
STAND

AND TOGETHER
WE FINISH.
GLORY
BE TO
JAH
ONE
CREATOR.
KEEP
THE
SPEAR
BURNING
ONE
LOVE
PEACE
BURNING SPEAR

(4PAN1T1PKSTC.E1) 4 Panel Digipak hdd 1/15/02

Burning Spear, *Our Music*, 2005
Album packaging for Burning
Music Productions
Pen and ink

Elvis Costello,
The Delivery Man, 2004
Album packaging and liner notes
for Lost Highway Records
Pen on paper

BUTTON MY LIP

01

Don't want to talk about the government
Don't want to talk about some incident
Don't want to talk about some peppermint gum
Don't want to talk about the time to come

Button my lip
'Til I'm smart enough

Don't raise your hand
'Cos I'm not offering
It serves you right
Now you are suffering
Give me a chance
To see it though
It all depends on what you hold is true

Button my lip
With your kiss

Don't want to hear some little sniveling
You just don't get what I'm delivering
Maybe you want me
But you know you can't
I'd say, "I want you"
But you know I don't

Button my lip
'Til I'm old enough
'Til I'm smart enough
'Til I'm...
Button my lip

Don't want to come at your beckoning
For any day they'll be a reckoning
Don't want to hear what is impossible
Baby you've become invisible

Button my lip

I've seen those clowns vacant and insolent
I stand accused but I am innocent
I am the mighty and magnificent

E.C.	Steve Nieve	Davey Faragher	Pete Thomas
VOCALS AND GIBSON SUPER 400 GUITAR	UPRIGHT PIANO	GIBSON EB1 BASS	DRUMS

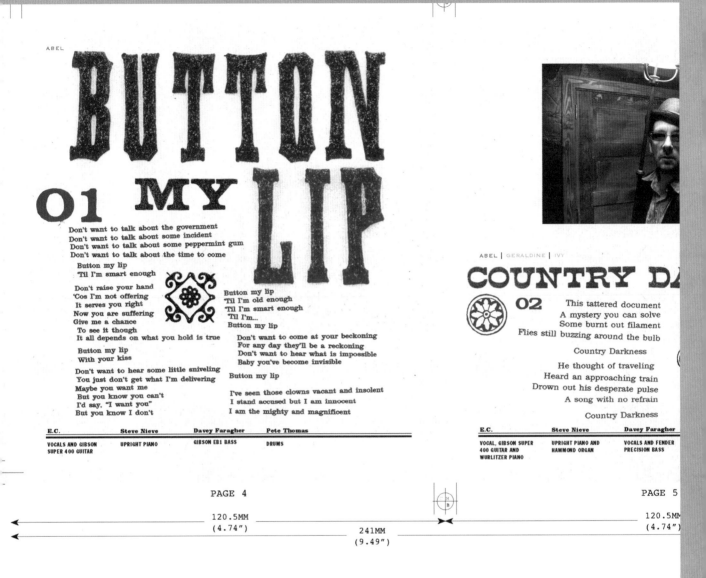

COUNTRY DA[RKNESS]

02

This tattered document
A mystery you can solve
Some burnt out filament
Flies still buzzing around the bulb

Country Darkness

He thought of traveling
Heard an approaching train
Drown out his desperate pulse
A song with no refrain

Country Darkness

E.C.	Steve Nieve	Davey Faragher
VOCAL, GIBSON SUPER 400 GUITAR AND WURLITZER PIANO	UPRIGHT PIANO AND HAMMOND ORGAN	VOCALS AND FENDER PRECISION BASS

PAGE 4

120.5MM
(4.74")

241MM
(9.49")

PAGE 5

120.5MM
(4.74")

The DELIVERY MAN

119.5MM
(4.71")

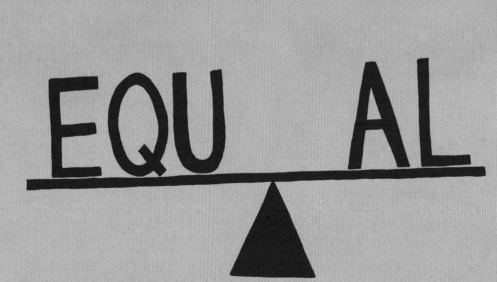

The Deadly Mexican
Halloween Fest, 2005
Poster
Silks creen

Equal, 2006
Drawing
Pen on paper

Why Hand, 2006
Poster
Pen on paper

APPLES ARE SUNBATHING

For the Loveworn, 2004
Snail-inspired sketch for a
promotional postcard
Pen on paper

Apples Are Sunbathing, 2005
Poster
China ink and square-tip brush

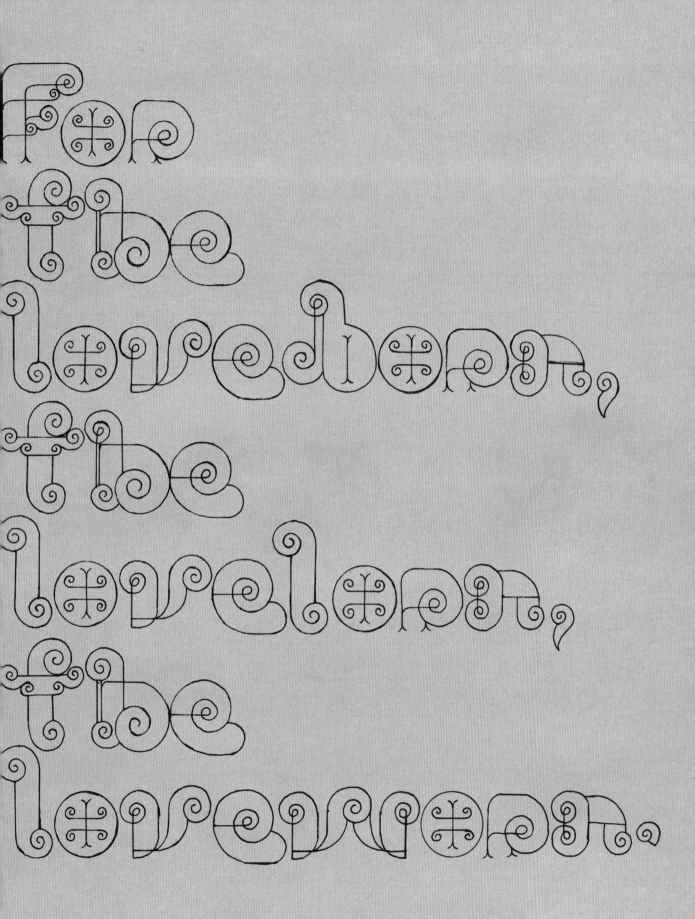

For
the
loveborn,
the
lovelorn,
the
loveworn.

Music for Lovers, 2006
Sticker
Offset printing

Morr Music Logotype, 2006
Flyer
Offset printing

Isan, 2006
Isan tour poster for Morr Music
Offset printing

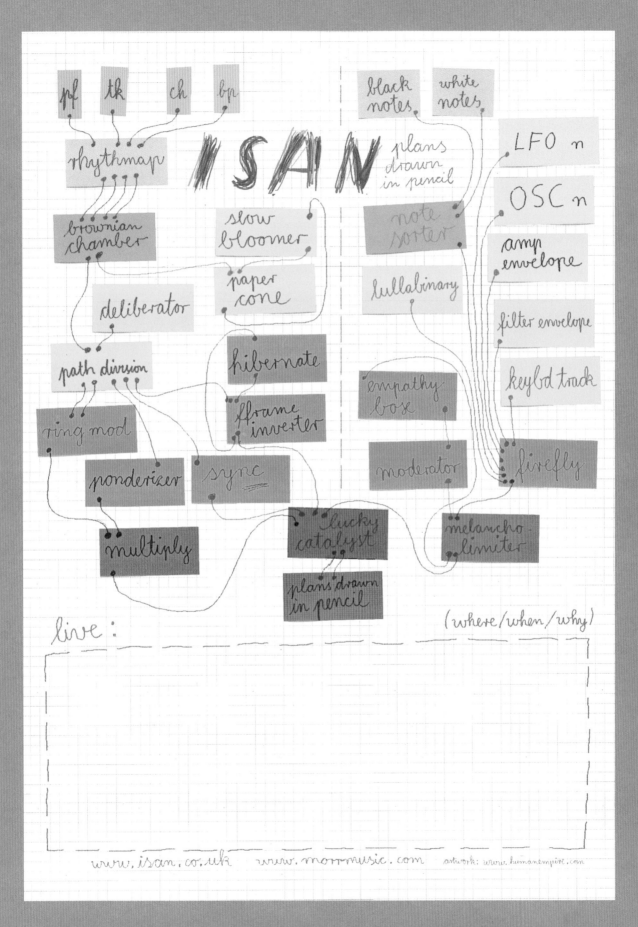

Populous, *Queue for Love*, 2006
LP cover for Morr Music
Offset printing

F.S.Blumm, *Zweite Meer*, 2005
LP cover for Morr Music
Offset printing

A
1. still in this town
2. statements
3. many frames per moment
4. throwing thoughts
5. trick or treat
B 6. who was first
7. afraid
8. even when it's not
9. a brief encounter
10. no need to mention
11. two minds inbetween

PROMO COPY

gut8er sundet

gut8er sundet

ISAN

06.2006
morr 068
drawn
in
pencil
cd/lp

05.2006
morr 059
a.r.c. dvd+cd

06.2006
morr 060
S/T cd

06.2006
morr 061
EA1/EA2 cd

TiED &
TICKLED TRIO

05.2006
morr 066
slow
days
cd/lp

the year of

COUCH

06.2006
morr 087
figur 5
cd/lp

COUCH
COUCH
COUCH

TheYear

ELECTRIC

ELECTRIC
PRESIDENT

ELECTRIC
PRESIDENT

Of

06.2006 / anost 009 / 7"
You Have The Right To
Remain Awesome: Vol. 1

06.2006 / anost 010 / 7"
You Have The Right To
Remain Awesome: Vol. 2

PRESIDENT

www.morrmusic.com

uther, *Sundet*, 2006
romotional-cd cover for Morr
usic
ffset

orr Music, *New Releases*, 2006
oster for Morr Music new releases
ffset

Benjamin Gibbard/Andrew Kenny lp, 2005
morr music berlin
leaves & berries

Electric President lp, 2005
morr music berlin
computer drawin

Morr Music poster, 2005
morr music
computer drawing

Morr Music poster, 2005
morr music
computer drawing

Jim the Illustrator, a.k.a. Jim Stoten, studied
at University of Brighton for three years and
then moved to London. He joined up with
Heart Agency in October 2005. Recently Jim
completed his first graphic novel, titled *The
Diamond* and is now looking for a publisher.
His work has been featured in *Amelias*
magazine, *Dazed and Confused*, *Cream*, *Beat*,
and *Gomez*.

London-based graphic artist and illustrator
Adrian Johnson was born in 1974 in Liverpool,
home of the Beatles, caustic wit, and petty
crime—all of which have influenced or affected
him in one way or another. He has exhibited in
New York, Singapore, and London and continues to work for a diverse range of clients across
varying disciplines. He occasionally lectures
across the U.K. and is currently designing
T-shirts for 2K By Gingham.

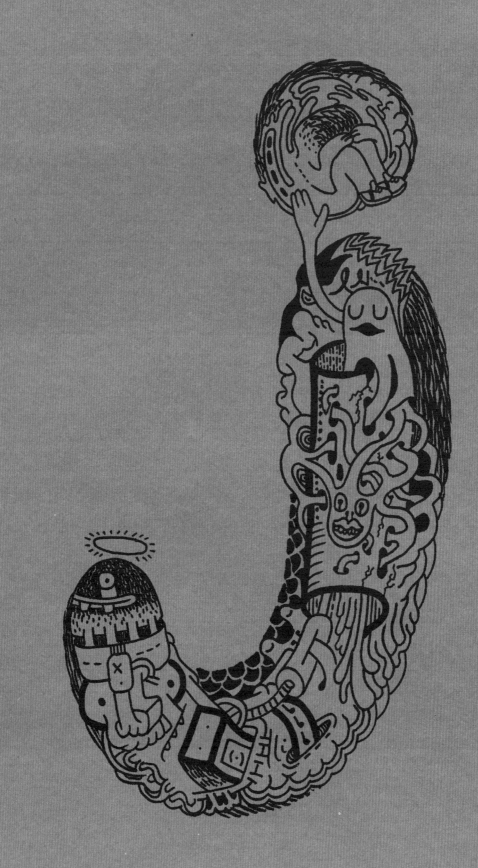

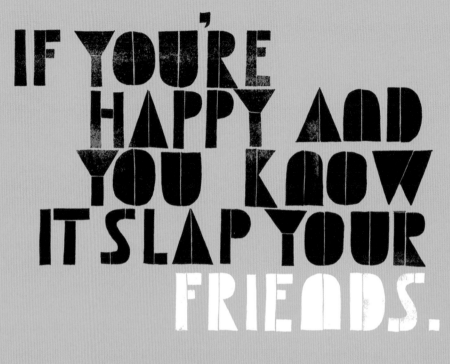

IF YOU'RE HAPPY AND YOU KNOW IT SLAP YOUR FRIENDS.

Slap Your Friends, 2005
T-shirt design
Pencil, paper, scanner, Apple G5

Olaf, 2005
Poster, one in a series titled
The Pillage People
Pencil, paper, scanner, Apple G5

Myfest, 2005
Poster
Pen on paper

Things Alphabet, 2005
Typeface
Pen on paper

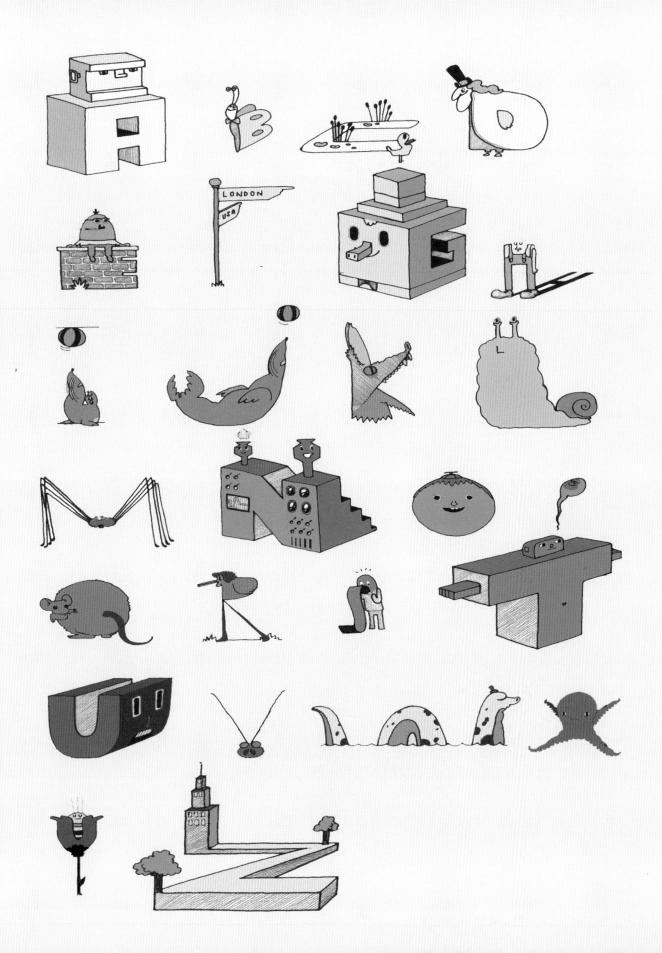

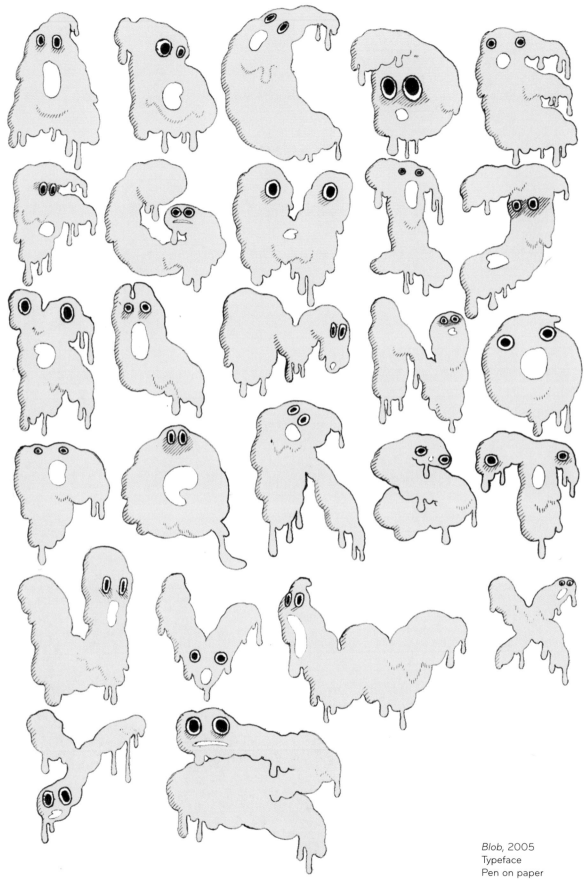

Blob, 2005
Typeface
Pen on paper

KAYROCK!

Kayrock Screenprinting was always more ambitious than your average silk screeners and art collectives. From the beginning, the duo of Karl Larocca (a.k.a. Kayrock, a.k.a. Pre-Raphaelite Shaolin) and Jef Scharf (a.k.a. Wolfy, a.k.a. Little Giant Robot Zero)—their name derived from the Wu-Tang Clan name generator—were tackling big subjects. By making catchy, infectious, psychedelic, Japanese, childlike posters for Oneida and Nada Surf, Kayrock Screenprinting became a big hit in their New York neighborhood, Williamsburg, setting the stage for bigger things. Kayrock and Wolfy decided to incorporate and hone their skills in screenprinting to provide the highest quality work possible. Chris Millstein recently joined the fold, bringing with him his expertise in hand-to-hand combat and T-shirt printing.

j. zachary keenan
www.j-zachary.com

J. Zachary Keenan's list: headphones, picture books, neckties, bass guitars, single-speed bicycles, audio and video, wallpaper, 1977, electricity, bent plywood, light-rail transit, snow, backpacks, sculpture, brothers, Indian food, posters, MP3s, Detroit, safety gear, laptops, beards, short stories, dogs, Capricorn, sketchbooks, the BBC, apartment life, keyboards, and Minneapolis.

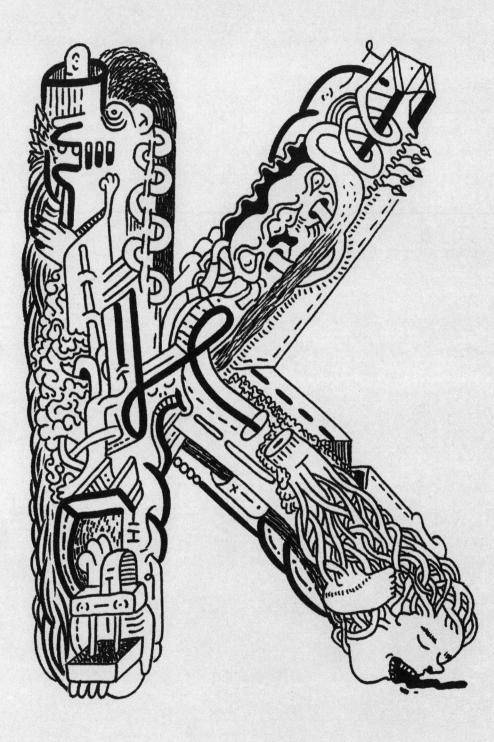

Company, 2004
Poster
Silk screen on paper

Dynasty, 2004
Poster
Silk screen on paper

Golden, 2002
Poster
Silk screen on paper

Untitled, 2004
Poster
Ink drawing on paper

The SQEEGEE

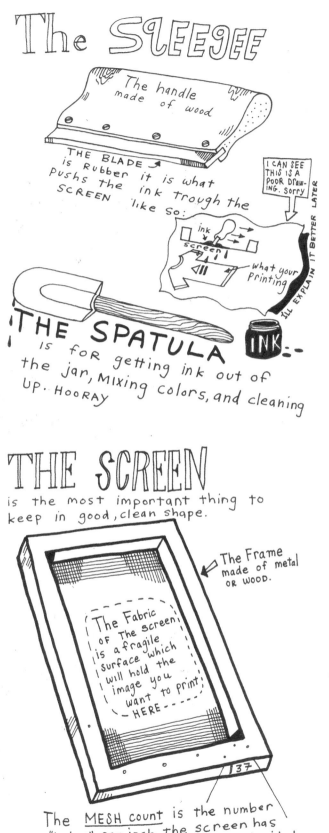

The handle made of wood

THE BLADE is Rubber it is what Pushs the ink trough the SCREEN like so:

ink
screen
what your Printing

I CAN SEE THIS IS A POOR DRAWING. SORRY

I'll EXPLAIN IT BETTER LATER

INK

THE SPATULA
IS FOR getting ink out of the jar, Mixing colors, and cleaning UP. HOORAY

Silkscreening with

WOLFY FROM KAYROCK
www.kayrock.org

THIS LITTLE BOOK WILL FAMILIARISE YOU WITH SOME OF THE STRANGE TOOLS AND TERMS WE'LL USE

Silkscreening dates back to ancient Japanese paper stencilling. The Process we are going to learn was patented in the early 1900s by Sam Simon in Manchester England. He printed for William Morris who is a super designer of patterns, wallpaper, chairs and all kinds of things. He is worth looking up if you have a chance. In 1914, John Pilsworth made the whole process what we know and love. He was from San Francisco. No one has ever made screen printing a clean process so please wear CLOTHES That you can work in and get inky!

THE SCREEN
is the most important thing to keep in good, clean shape.

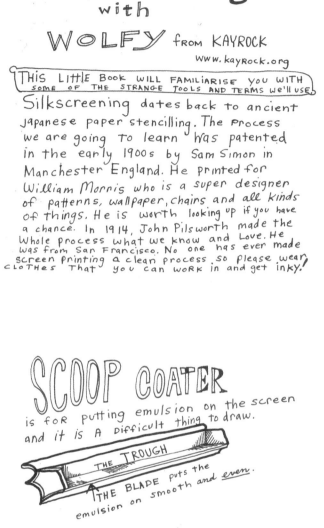

The Frame made of metal OR WOOD.

The Fabric of The screen is a fragile surface which will hold the image you want to print — HERE —

37

The MESH count is the number OF "holes" per inch the screen has higher counts are FOR more detailed work and Lower is good for large areas of color.

SCOOP COATER
is FOR putting emulsion on the screen and it is A difficult thing to draw.

THE TROUGH
THE BLADE puts the emulsion on smooth and even.

EMULSION is what blocks the "holes" in the screen. IT is photo sensitive and allows you to put the image on the screen so that ink only comes out where you want it too. This is the Part where we literally work in the dark or, well, with a red "party" bulb. Emulsion is usually a Pretty color like blue oR Purple oR even yellow. The process of putting the image on the screen is called **BURNING** but it doesn't us. any fire.

Bad Touch, 2001
Poster
Silk screen on paper

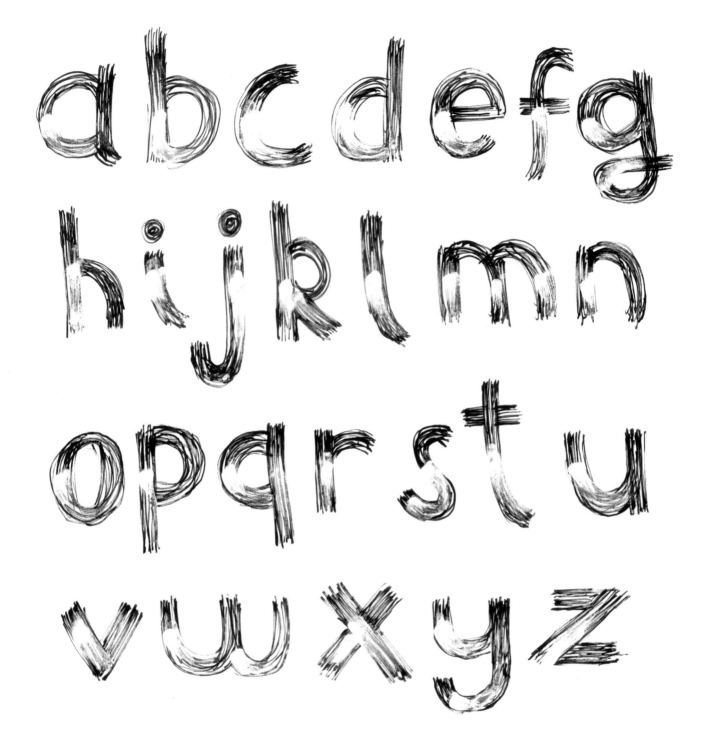

Okay, Okay…Alright, 2006
Type study for Okay, Alright
typeface
Sharpie paint markers

JEFFREY LAI

www.jeffreylai.info

Jeff Lai's parents bought him a computer when he was eight years old. He used to spend hours on MS Paint, trying to master the drawing tool. Jeff followed this effort by studying at the University of Wisconsin, followed by Minneapolis College of Art and Design, then the University of Brighton and Yale University. He has a studio in Brooklyn, where he works on both self-initiated and client projects. He is now in his first semester teaching at City University of New York.

Lifelong friendship society
lifelongfriendshipsociety.com

Lifelong Friendship Society (LFS) is a collective company comprised of creative directors, artists, designers, animators, writers, and musicians. LFS thrives on personal anarchy that translates into a larger, freewheeling whole. It takes on a variety of projects, including motion graphics, print design, exhibitions, and self-created content.

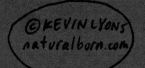

© KEVIN LYONS
naturalborn.com

Kevin Lyons is a 1992 graduate of the Rhode Island School of Design, where he received a degree in film. After working for Nickelodeon/MTV as an associate producer, he cofounded a New York City–based design firm called Stereo-type. After receiving his master's degree in design from CalArts in 1996, Kevin went on to work for Nike and Spike Jonze's Girl Skateboards Company. During the 1990s he maintained freelance clients, and in 2000 Kevin was named one of the "top forty designers under thirty" by I.D. magazine. For three years, Kevin worked as the art director for the quirky, urban Japanese magazine *Tokion*. He was next the art director for Urban Outfitters and most recently was design director for Stussy. He now lives in Philadelphia, where he maintains a small experimental project and company called Natural Born.

Each business card reads:

New York, NY
646.322.0153
mail@jeffreylai.info
www.jeffreylai.info

Business cards, 2005
Business cards
Two-color offset printing and marker

I Participated, 2003
T-shirt
Screenprint T-shirt

JEFFREY LAI IS WILLING
TO GIVE ONE PERSON
$50
WHO HAS A GREAT
IDEA ON HOW TO
HIGHLIGHT their
FAVORITE BOOKS,
MUSIC & MOVIES
in the YALE UNIVERSITY
LIBRARY
SYSTEM
I PARTICIPATED
* All ideas
must be documented
and emailed to:
jeffrey.lai@yale.edu
EVERYBODY WHO PARTICIPATES
WILL GET THIS FREE T-Shirt
SEE ALL ENTRIES
AND ADDITIONAL
INFORMATION
AT
isongard.
yale.edu/
~jeffreylai/
50dollars

Sex Mess, 2005
An illustration
Mixed media

Favorite Sons, 2005
A logo for the band Favorite Sons
Pen on paper

Hacksaw, 2005
T-shirt
Metal

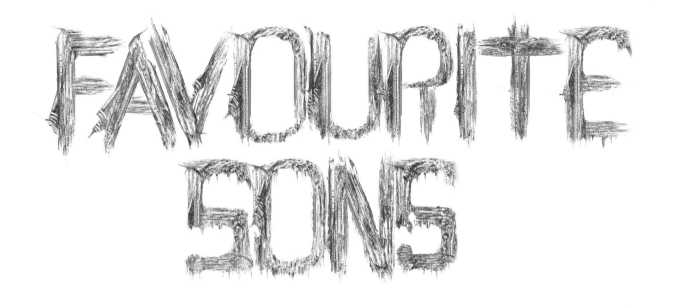

FAVOURITE SONS

HACKSAW KOBE GRETSKY

I, 2005
Shell chair for Modernica X Arkitip
Acrylic on fiberglass

Kokura Chapter, 2005
Stussy Japan T-shirt drawing
Ink on paper

STEFAN MARX
LIVINCOMPANY.COM

Stefan Marx is a drawer. He was born in 1979 and lives in Hamburg, Germany. The first and the last thing in his day is drawing. He tries to describe his world, his thoughts, and his views on the real world with his drawings and paintings. Stefan publishes small zines that include his works and thoughts, which derive from his love of sketchbooks and all things in books. In addition, Stefan runs a small label called The Lousy Livincompany, where he produces T-shirt designs in small editions so that his friends can wear them too.

GEOFF MCFETRIDGE
championdontstop.com

Geoff McFetridge is a graphic artist based in Los Angeles, California. He creates work for clients within the traditional world of graphic design as well as on projects that test those boundaries of his job description. This unbounded approach to doing design is a definitive aspect of his work. After graduating with an MFA from the California Institute of the Arts he became art director for *Grand Royal Magazine* from 1995 to 1997. Although at first glance he appears only to have himself as a client, he has a stellar list of clients: Patagonia, Stussy, Burton Snowboards, Marc Jacobs, Lignet Roset, Milk Fed, Girl Skateboards, Hermes, and Greenpeace

Nicole M. Michels
Bird and Banner.com

Nicole Michels is co-owner of Bird and Banner, a design studio that specializes in custom and hand-printed invitations and announcements. She currently divides her time between Philadelphia and Lancaster, Pennsylvania, where she lives with her husband and dog.

Patrick Miller
www.faile.net

Regarded by many as a very pleasant guy, Patrick Miller has a natural love for doodling and recording his thoughts visually. His sketchbooks show a stream-of-consciousness style of drawing that naturally incorporates typography and image. While in school at the Minneapolis College of Art and Design, he started the art team Faile with Patrick McNeil and Aiko Nakagawa. Now based in New York, Faile shows its work internationally. Miller, with McNeil, also started Our Design Company, where they work for the design, film, music, and fashion industries.

Chris Millstein

Chris Millstein is an artist and printmaker who lives and works in Brooklyn. He has designed and silk-screened posters and record covers, by hand, since the early 1990s. His work has been exhibited in Berlin, London, Tokyo, and of course the United States. When not working creatively and technically with Kayrock and Wolfy, he can be found playing drums with the bands Home, Jah Division, and Charter Oak.

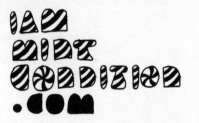

Mint Condition is the experimental forest of a twenty-three-year-old Minnesota native, designer Travis Stearns (He reps Minnesota). In December of 2006, Travis will graduate with a B.A. and honors in graphic design from the College of Design at North Carolina State University, after which he would like to work in a collaborative environment with a range of music, fashion, and cultural institutions. Some of his interests include design history, needlepoint alphabets, camouflage patterns, Scandinavian folk art, the 1987 Minnesota Twins, and Dutch typography.

Garrett Morin was born twenty-five years ago in Massachusetts and began drawing soon after. 2004, Garrett graduated from the Rhode Island School of Design and, after working briefly in Los Angeles, moved to Brooklyn, where he currently resides. Garrett does freelance art and design for Rad Mountain. His work has appeared in publications such as Flaunt, Complex, The Drama, and Swindle. Past clients include MTV, Cingular, and Red Bull.

kindra murphy
knickknackreport.com
kindramurphy.com

Kindra Murphy is an assistant professor at the Minneapolis College of Art and Design, where she teaches graphic design. She also designs college catalogs and educational materials for young audiences, as well as gallery materials for a number of nonprofit organizations. Before teaching at MCAD, she worked for Urban Outfitters, the Walker Art Center, and Maine College of Art. Kindra is constantly gathering printed ephemera, documenting the everyday and creating fun bits for her design work.

SMALL VILLE

HOUSE PATCH

SMALLVILLE

SLEEPARCHIVE LIVE (BERLIN)
STEN (DIAL/SMALLVILLE)
JULIUS STEINHOFF (SMALLVILLE)
RENÉ DACHNER (WEALD)

28.4.2006 – 24H – UEBEL & GEFÄHRLICH

SMALLVILLE-RECORDS.COM

Smallville, 2005
Logo for a Hamburg record store
and record label
Marker, typewriter, and drawing

House Patch, 2005
House patch packaging
House font

Smallville Flyer Sleeparchive, 200
Flyer
Ink-drawn letters, offset printing

The Lousy Livincompany, 2005
Poster, edition of 500
Drawing

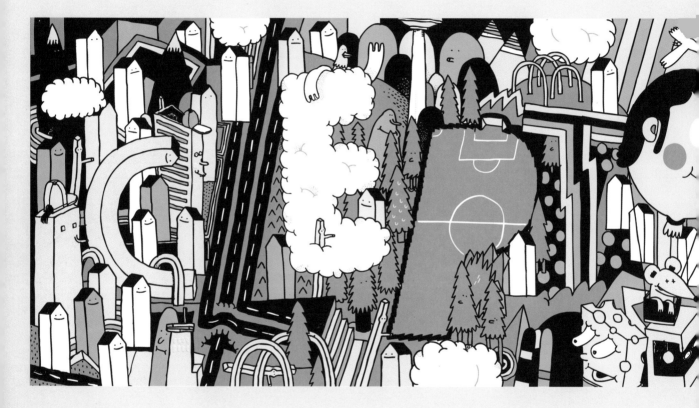

Cleptomanicx Elbnessi, 2005
Skateboard deck
Drawing pen and ink

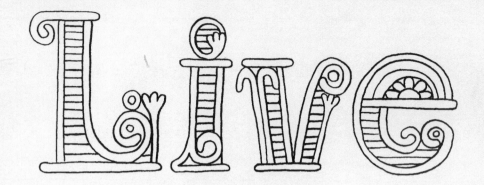

none (live what you love), 2006
Patagonia
Pencil drawing for T-shirt design

Boredom, 2003
Faile Book Project
Pen

DON'T BE BORED.

TRY TO VISUALIZE CATASTROPHE. NOT
MERELY THE INEVITABILITY OF DEATH
BUT THE TERRIBLE THINGS THAT
WILL HAPPEN TO YOU BEFORE YOU DIE.

LET'S
SHARE.

I mean... you could get
hit by a car tomorrow.

Really, Really, Really...

Not the
kind of place
you get your
heart broken.

I WOULDN'T
WORRY
ABOUT IT.

Even in a room
full of people
you may still
feel lonely.

?...

I
TOLD
YOU
THAT
ALREADY.

SOMEONE I MET... I CAN'T
REMEMBER HIS NAME.

Above You, 2006
The Whitest Boy Alive, Album
Package
Pencil drawing for poster

Party invitation, 2002
Milk Fed
Pencil drawing for a party invitation

Album Cover (album: Masterpiece),
2004
Rip Slyme
Pencil drawing for T-shirt design

Let's share, 2003
Self
Pen drawing for T-shirt design

Landscape, 2006
Patagonia,
Pencil drawing

Patagonia, 2006
Patagonia,
Ribon and Pen

Untitled, 2005
Typeface
Pen on paper

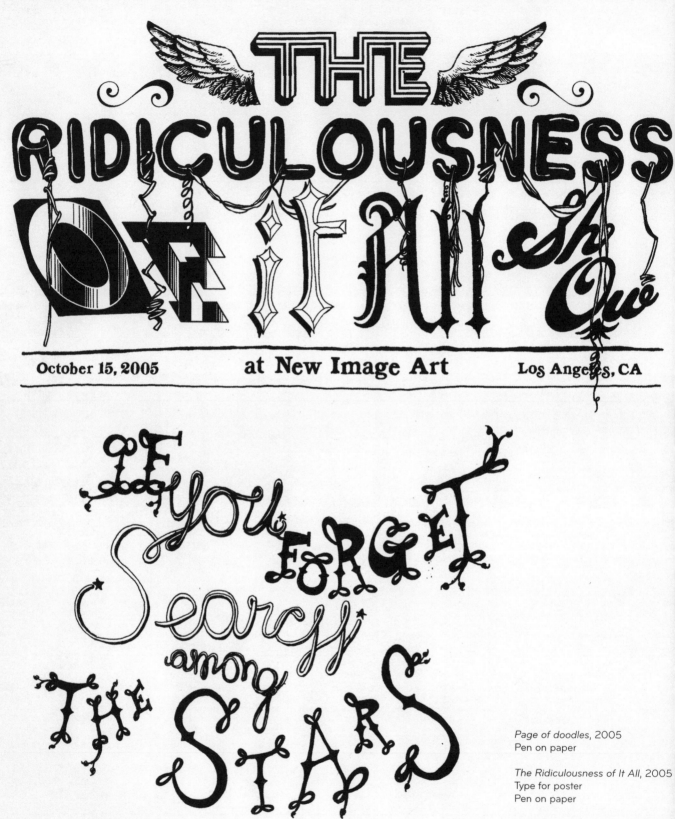

THE RIDICULOUSNESS OF IT ALL Show

October 15, 2005 at New Image Art Los Angeles, CA

IF you FORGET Search among THE STARS

Page of doodles, 2005
Pen on paper

The Ridiculousness of It All, 2005
Type for poster
Pen on paper

If You Forget Search Among the
Stars, 2004
Idea
Pen on paper

Shears, 2006
Sketches for the salon Shears
Pen on paper

Untitled (page 162-163), 2004
Random sketchbook doodles
Pen and marker on paper

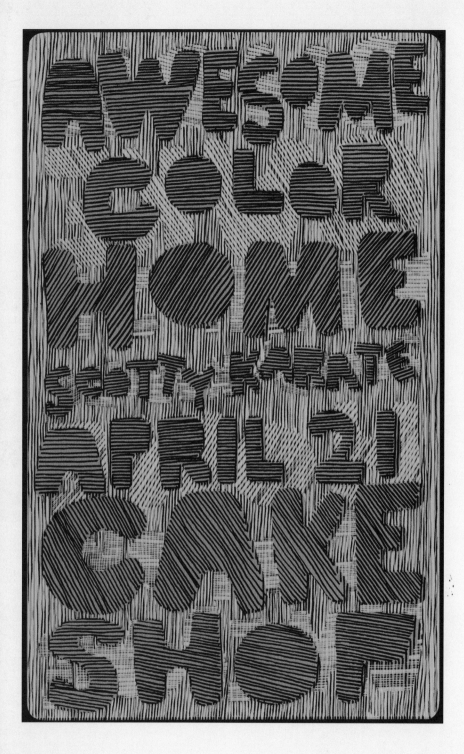

Home/Awesome Color, 2006
Poster
Two-color silk screen on 80-poun[
black Pegasus cover stock

Social Registry, 2005
Poster
Two-color silk screen on 100-pou[
Cougar cover stock

Home/Leels, 2006
Poster
Two-color silk screen on 100-pou[
Cougar cover stock

FROM THE TOP
OF THE MAP

Young Tizzle, 2006
Typographic experiment
Young Jeezy song on repeat, bezi
yays in Adobe Illustrator

Art Works, Why Don't You?, 2006
Wall drawing and installation
Zig Painty markers, acrylic paint,
1980s music (for inspiration)

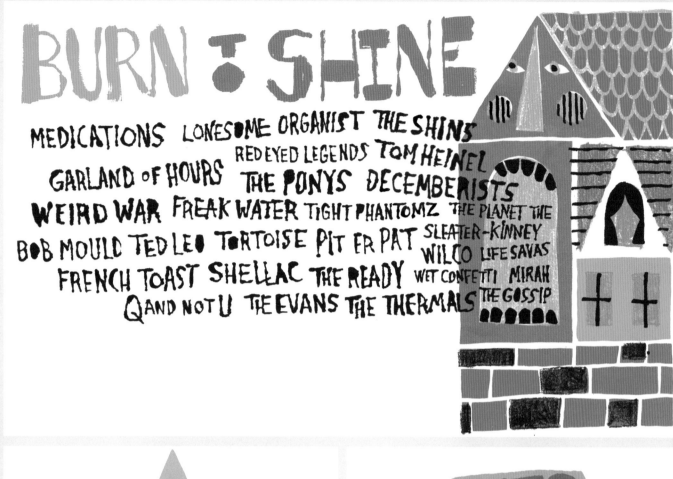

Burn to Shine, 2006
Title illustration for *Swindle*
magazine
Pen on paper

Auto Bodies, 2006
Title illustration for *Swindle*
magazine
Mixed materials

Rad Mountain, 2005
Rad Mountain logo
Pen on paper

Sleep Spell, 2006
Poster
Two-color silk screen

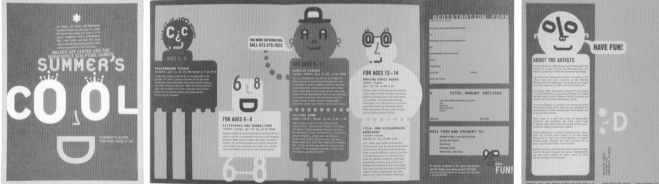

Artwork of the Month (Jacques Lipchitz), 2001
Walker Art Center
Hand drawn type

Summer's Cool, 1999
Walker Art Center
Type People from Emigré's platelet

Free First Saturday, 2005
Type Study for Walker Art Center
Plaster letters and opaque projector

2 x 2, 2005
Colorforms

Feel Good, 2003
Kindra's calling card
Found signage

Artwork of the Month, 2000
Walker Art Center
Hand-drawn type

feel good

feel good

GET INTO THE SWING!

ARIKIDEA
MARK DI SUVERO

JUNE 2000   WALKER ART CENTER   ARTWORK OF THE MONTH   MINNEAPOLIS SCULPTURE GARDEN

M M ᵀ⁰ LANG L∩ LANGUAGE

B OBJECT
→ [M-W]

OUR OBJECT [W-M] [] [M

OF YOUR R

WEEK 12345
WEEK ONE TWO

1 99

URBN.COM URBAN OUTFITTERS
URBAN OUTFITTERS
+ PU

→ BASIC SCHE

[WE

Y[] WELCOME !

ALL are welcome

Kathy
NICCO

graphiddesigninternsip I(('I998 99-I9
I(((I9998

my Label   Extended Label
Extended Label

HOW TO
READ A
LABE

WALKER ART CENTER
walkerARTcenter
WALKERartCENTER
walker art CENTer

grapic
des
ign
INTERNsh
ip

Center*
of contemporary art,
month internship
(full-time)
epartment.
esponsibility for
tionalmaterials for
ual arts
forming arts,
m/video,
cation, and
bership programs.
iency ((Quark
Photoshop,
Illustrator)))
aphic skills,and
print production reqired.
TEREST in contemporary arts
nd current cultural trends desired.
ith clients and be able tomeet
tight deadlines.

a BFA or MFA degree in
ed to apply by
JUNE I5,.I998.

free
yes it's free
free

:00 pm

Steven Harrington

Justin Krietemeyer

NATIONALFOREST.COM

National Forest is a full-service creative think tank
with an expertise in execution. It creates visual
languages that can last a season or a lifetime.
The art directors, designers, photographers, and
receptionists apply their respective artistic
backgrounds, love of culture, and collaborative
approach to every endeavor. Although
National Forest firmly believes that the concept
is the foundation of any effective campaign, it is
dedicated to developing and reinventing aesthetics and approaches to move its work forward
graphically.

WWW.NEITHERFISHNORFOWL.COM

Neither Fish Nor Fowl is Jim Datz, a multidis-
ciplinary designer and illustrator who recently
moved to London, following four years as
art director of the Urban Outfitters Web and
Catalog division. Raised on the beaches of
southern New Jersey and a steady diet of
skating, surfing, listening to punk rock, and
taunting non-locals, he eventually decamped
to Philadelphia to study architecture at the
University of Pennsylvania. During a summer in
Japan, he was bitten hard by the fast-forward-
culture bug and returned home with a headful
of ideas, abandoning a promising career to
play in the fields of the superficial and trendy.
It was a really, really good decision.

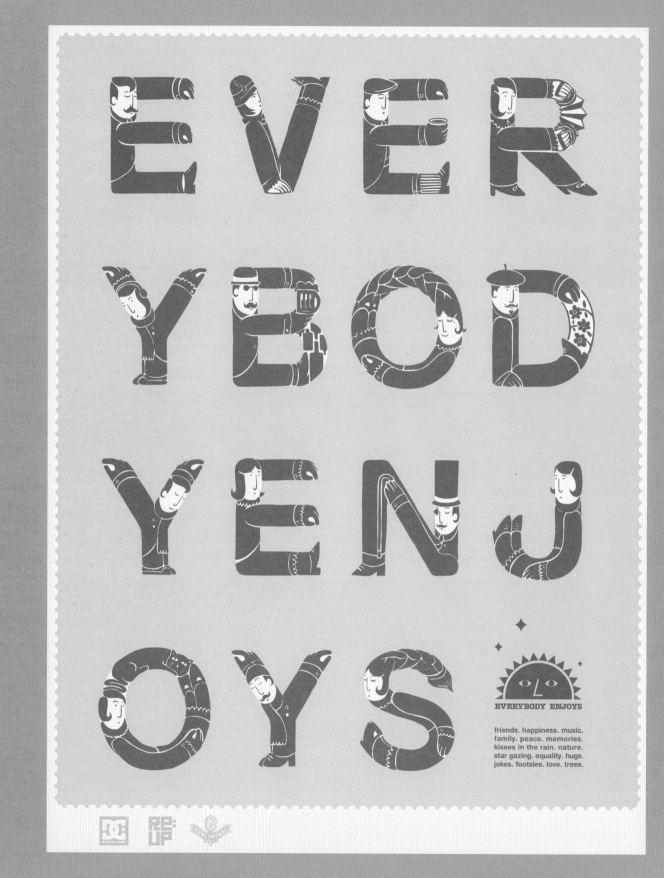

EVER
YBOD
YENJ
OYS

EVERYBODY ENJOYS

friends. happiness. music.
family. peace. memories.
kisses in the rain. nature.
star gazing. equality. hugs.
jokes. footsies. love. trees.

...erybody Enjoys, 2004
...oster
...lk screen

...arlight series, 2005
...ateboards for Element
...ateboards
...lk screen

Paint Love, 2006
Type for Element Skateboards
logo and slogan
Silk screen

Thank You, 2006
Art show
Process photo

Listen to the Trees, 2005
Illustration for *Rockpile*
magazine
Ink on napkin, found
photograph

Untitled, 2005
Stickers for Urban Outfitters
Digitally manipulated ink
drawing

Seven Seas, 2004
Personal project
Digitally manipulated ink drawing

Casual Domestic, 2004
Personal project
Digitally manipulated ink drawing

Sweet Tooth, 2003
Applied graphic for Urban
Outfitters packaging
Digitally manipulated ink drawing

Untitled (Alphabets), 2004
Personal project
Scan from sketchbook

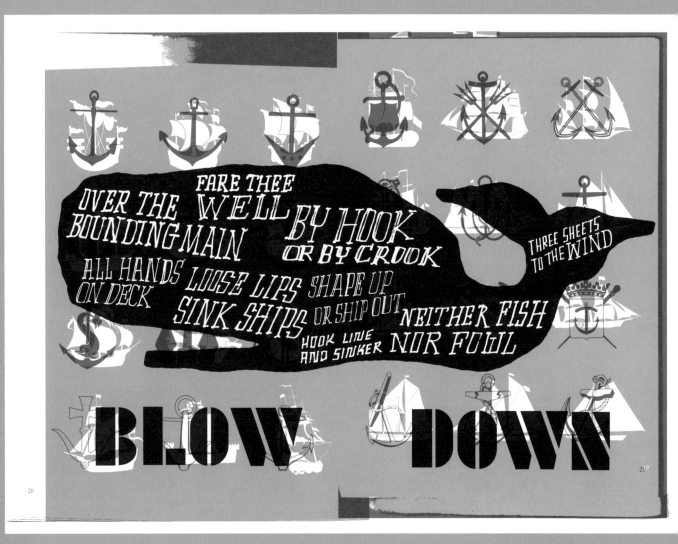

Blow Down, 2003
Poster for group show at Skatene▮
Minnow, edition of twenty
Archival ink jet print on tiled
steno paper

Come to Your Senses, 2006
Poster for Neither Fish Nor Fowl, ▮
in a series of six
Digitally manipulated ink drawing,
sampled textures

CD covers, 2004–05
Character design for Mixxclub
covers
Digitally manipulated ink drawing

Semaphore, 2005
Personal project
Digitally manipulated ink drawing

Anything and Everything, 2003–C
Selections from sketchbooks
Digitally manipulated ink drawing

A.J. PURDY
WWW.GRAPHDROME.COM

A.J. Purdy likes to travel but is really poor. He likes to share music but not watch TV. He drew way better when he was six years old. A.J. thinks of himself as a positive individual and appreciates people who prepare food for him. He really likes to collaborate with artists. He's been told by many people that he looks like other people they know. A.J. now lives in Italy but does not speak Italian, because he is a stupid American.

I Want Girls to Like Me, 2005
Miscellaneous drawing with
Imagination typeface
Pen and ink

Don't Touch Me, 2005
Miscellaneous drawing; Loch
typeface
Pen and ink

IF WE ALL TRIED REAL HARD WE COULD DESTROY THE WORLD

If We All Tried Real Hard We Could Destroy the World, 2005
Atdestroy
Pen and ink

Buttface, 2005
Miscellaneous drawing; type by Andy Rementer, drawing by A.J. Purdy
Pen and marker

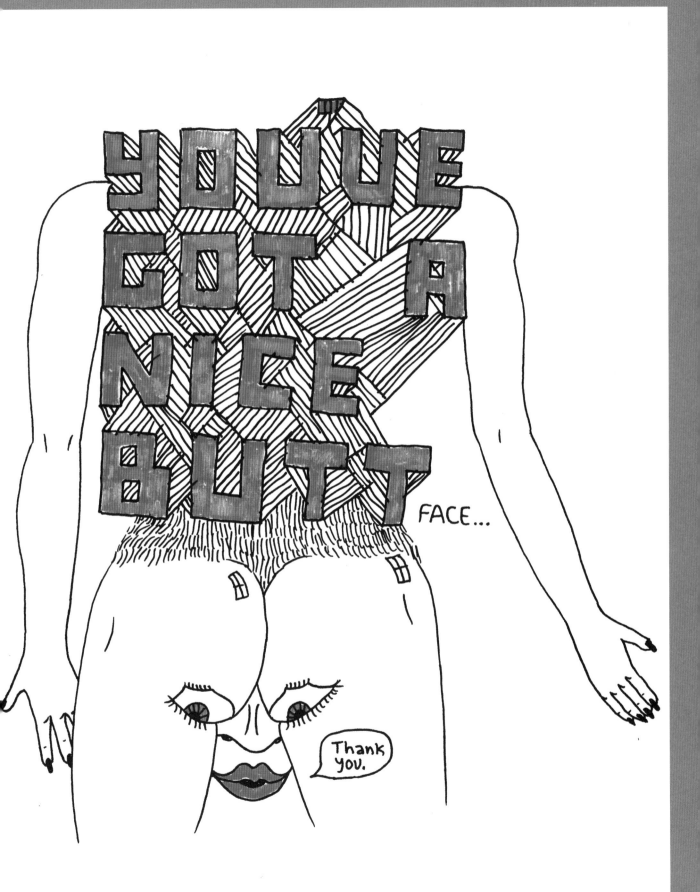

Luke Ramsey
www.anteism.com

Luke Ramsey has been making gig posters, zines, comics, installations, and murals for the past four years. In 2005, Luke had his first solo gallery show at Space 1026 in Philadelphia. He just finished a comic book, *Finding Joy*, and is currently working on the "me be me we be" collaborative drawing project. He and his partner, Angela, have started an artist residency in their home on Pender Island, British Columbia. Their residency promotes the "me be me we be" and encourages creativity and well-being among other collaborative artists.

Andy Rementer
www.andyrementer.com

Andy Rementer grew up in southern New Jersey in a quiet town once free of Wal-Marts and strip malls. After graduating from the University of the Arts in Philadelphia, Andy worked in New York City for various design and motion-graphics studios. As he became bored of the daily grind, he retreated into his sketchbooks, where he recovered a new world of drawing. Invigorated Andy found pleasure in making illustrations for stickers, T-shirts, and independent magazines. Eventually, his interests shifted toward comics, a medium that combines the worlds of drawing, graphic design, and storytelling. Inspiration for his work comes from the barrage of visual stimulation in the world, including the ugly side of pop culture, the isolation of technology, and the mainstream obsession with butts.

Royal & Remarkable™
www.royalremarkabletm.com

Royalremarkable Gajownik frequented North Carolina State University for six years. He went to study aerospace engineering but stayed for the graphic design. His work often starts with typography. He likes one-liners and 747s, although he's never been on one. His work can be seen at places like *Beautiful Decay* magazine and *Sekushi*, *NLF*—the magazine and the book, *Windhover*, *Grafuck*, *Rosebud*, *Arkitip*, and here, in this very book, of course. As you will see in subsequent visuals, he's a fairly successful and wealthy aerospace engineer.

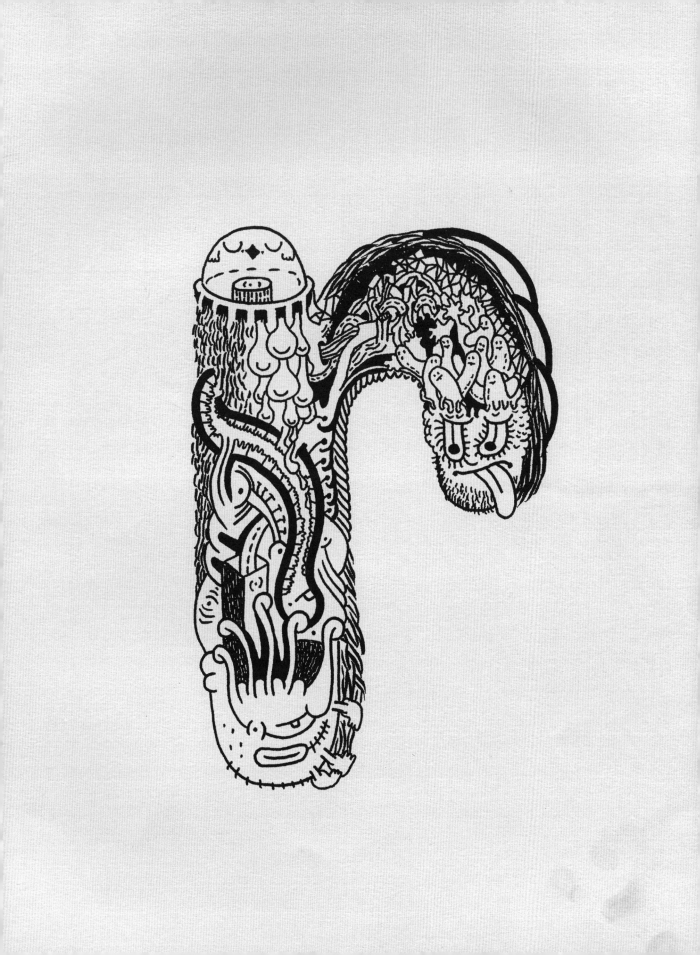

The Be Cause, 2004
Poster design for solo show,
Luke Ramsey 2004
Ink, paper collage, and color
on paper

Be Kind, 2005
Drawing for housewarming gift
Ink, watercolor on paper

Help Me Help Me, 2005
Drawing
Ink, gouache, watercolor
on paper

Be Do Be, 2005
Drawing for a collector
Ink, watercolor on paper

I Have Never Made Any Fucking
Money from My Art, 2006
Book illustration
Offset printing

Sugo #3, 2006
Magazine cover
Offset printing

QUIT BLU-BALL IN' ME.

YOU CANT MAKE ME WASH ANYTHING

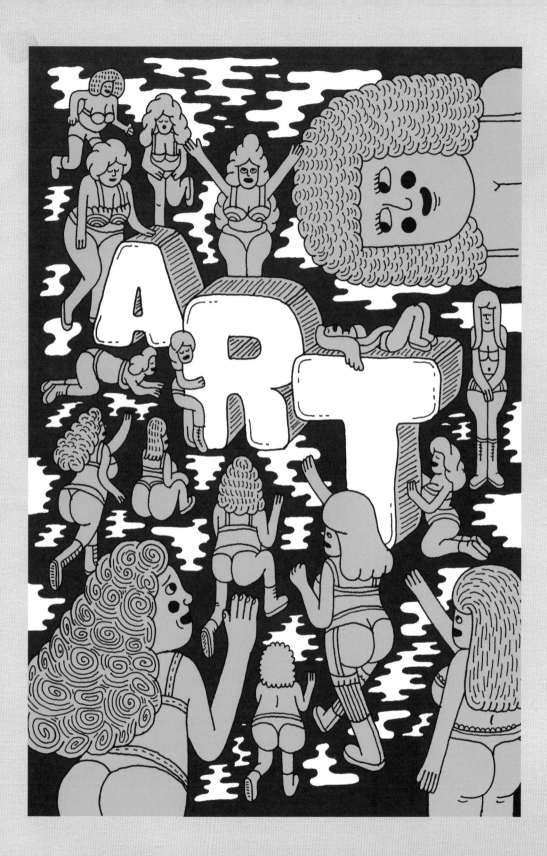

Sugo #3, 2006
Miscellaneous logos
Offset printing

Crib-Hop All-stars, 2005
Quilt
One-off printing on jersey, to be
sewn into a quilt

All We Do, 2005
Painting
Acrylic on found piece of wood

Labor Day Ain't Shit, 2005
Painting
Watercolor and ink on a Mac
OS X Tiger upgrade box

Nah v. Nature, 2005
Drawing
Ink on notebook paper,
digital color

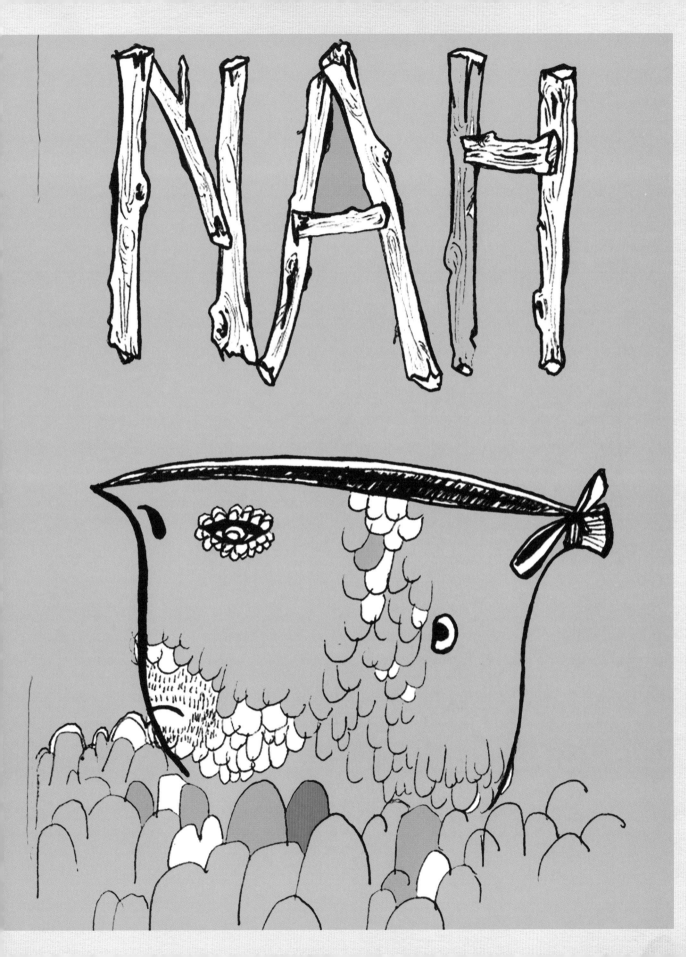

Sagmeister.com
STEFAN SAGMEISTER

Stefan Sagmeister formed the New York–based
Sagmeister Inc. in 1993 and has since
designed branding, graphics, and packaging for
clients as diverse as the Rolling Stones, HBO,
the Guggenheim Museum, and Time Warner.
Having been nominated five times for a Grammy
Award, he finally won one for the Talking Heads
boxed set. He has also earned practically every
important international design award.

ANDY SMITH
www.asmithillustration.com

Since graduating from London's Royal College
of Art, Andy Smith's work has been featured in
advertising campaigns, book jackets, editorials, animations, and interiors for clients such
as Nike, Expedia, Mercedes, Random House,
Orange, and Penguin Books, earning him
D&AD, AOI, and Creative Circle awards. His work
entails characters, humor, and events from his
immediate surroundings to create a visual world
that is all his own. Illustrations are combined
with strong typography and copywriting skills to
create work that speaks for itself.

Anthony Sheret
Workbylunch.com

Anthony Sheret is a nineteen-year-old graphic
designer and typographer who resides south of
London. He currently attends Brighton University,
where he studies graphic design.

Sam Sherman
samuel sherman.com

Sam Sherman graduated from Minneapolis
College of Art and Design in 2003. Currently
he lives and works in Minneapolis. He likes
form, vector formats, systems, and sequence.

TODD ST. JOHN

WWW.HUNTERGATHERER.NET

Todd St. John is a designer, animator, and
filmmaker living in New York City. Originally
from Hawaii, Todd grew up drawing and making
music. In 1994, while living in California, he co-
founded the independent label Green Lady with
Gary Benzel. Green Lady started out making
small runs of shirts and prints for friends, then
introduced a yearly series of designs, selling
to select stores primarily in the United States
and Japan. Todd later moved to New York and,
in 2000, founded HunterGatherer, a studio
focusing on conceptual work across a range of
mediums, mainly design, video, and film.

STRANGE ATTRACTORS
DESIGN

Ryan Pescatore Frisk and Catelijne van
Middelkoop are the founding partners of Strange
Attractors Design, an international studio special-
izing in typography and brand communication
for print, motion, and interactive media. They
have collaborated with clients, both cultural and
commercial, to design solutions and products
that represent distinct messages and experiences. Along with its professional work, the
studio gives workshops and lectures worldwide
and initiates autonomous projects, such as
Broadcasting Tongues, a study of graphic dialects

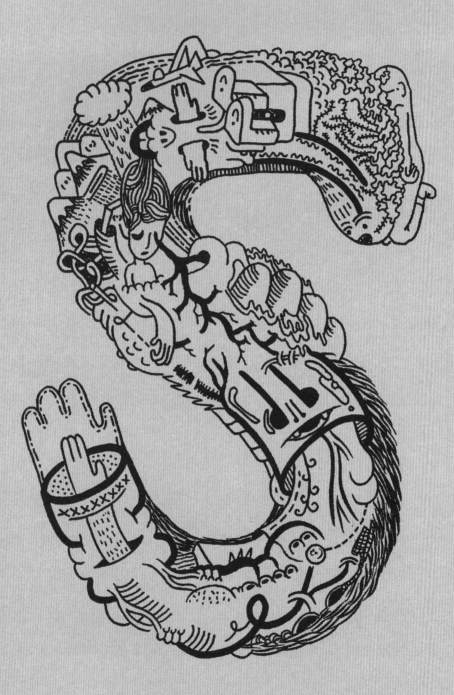

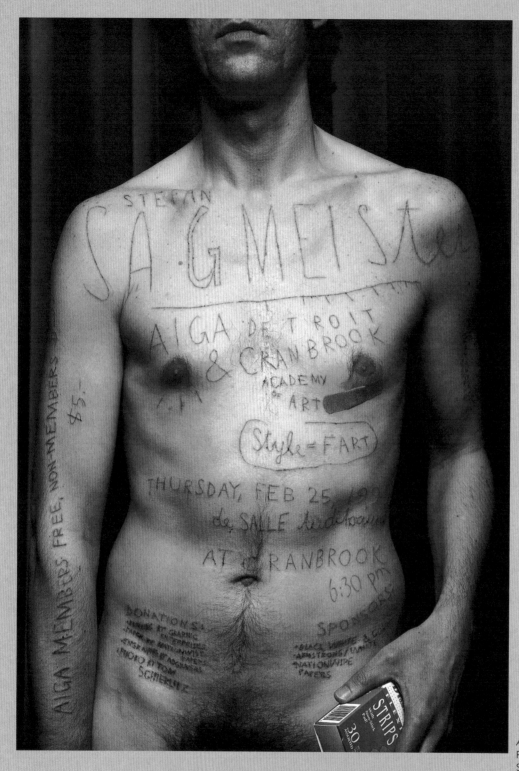

AIGA Detroit, 1999
Poster; art direction by Stefan Sagmeister, photography by Tod Schierlitz
Knife on skin

.Copy 4 Magazine, 2005
Art direction by Stefan Sagmeister, design by Traian Stanescu, photography by Oliver Meckes and Nicole Ottawa
Photograph

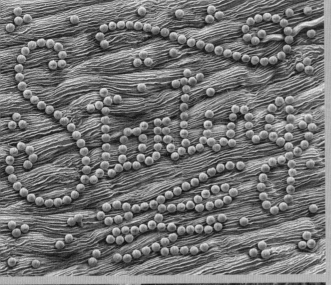

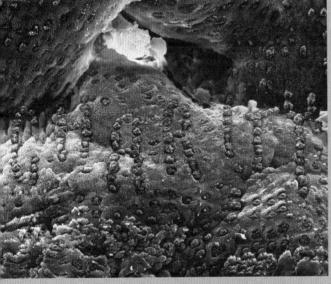

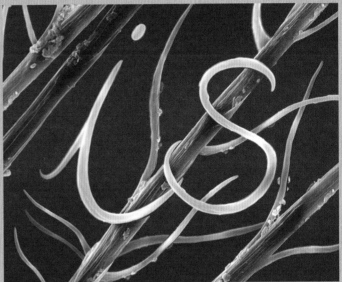

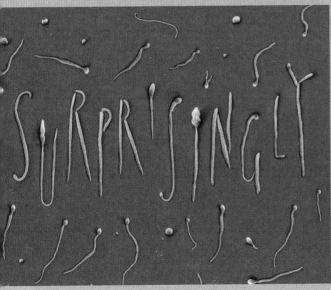

b the friendly letter

b says 'b lovely to see you again'
b says 'b lucky in your exams'
b says 'b a devil, come home early.'

'B' the Friendly Letter, 2003
Press advertisement for Orange
Digital

Datadump, 2006
Illustration for Fast Company
magazine
Digital printing

The Face of Disaster, 2000
Limited-edition poster
Silk screen print

Regrettably YES, 2005
Limited edition poster
Silk screen print

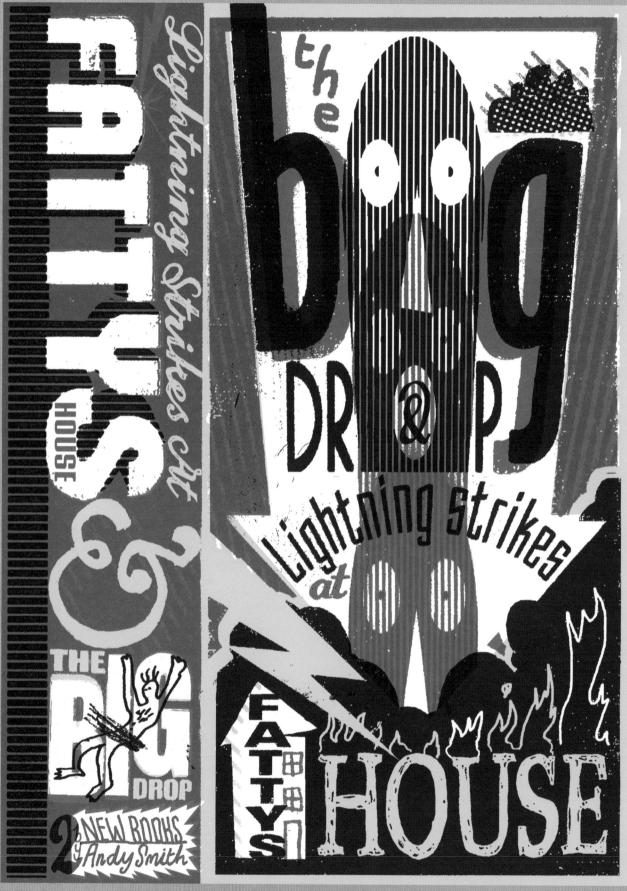

One Mans Junk is another man's TREASURE

The Big Drop and Lightning Strikes at Fattys House, 2004
Promotional poster for
self-published books
Silk screen print

One Man's Junk..., 2004
T-shirt design for Howies
Silk Screen print

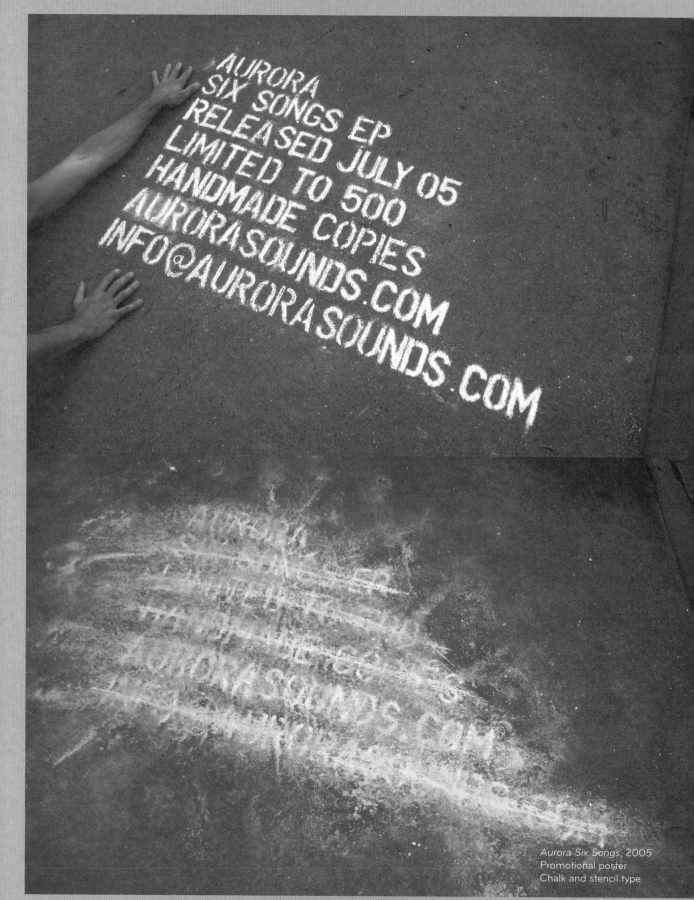

AURORA
SIX SONGS EP
RELEASED JULY 05
LIMITED TO 500
HANDMADE COPIES
AURORASOUNDS.COM
INFO@AURORASOUNDS.COM

Aurora Six Songs, 2005
Promotional poster
Chalk and stencil type

O.K., 2005
Quick logo sketch redrawn as a
vector image
Felt-tip marker

So Fresh, 2006
Sketch, redrawn as a vector imag[e]
Toothpaste

New Fangled, 2002
Installation object
Cut redwood

Nike Considered, 2005
Postcard, T-shirt, box design;
Manifesto typography
Silk screened hand-drawn type

Big Type Says More, 2006
Installation, custom drawn and
cut type; permanent collection,
Museum Boijmans Van Beuninge
Rotterdam, NL
Honeycomb cardboard panels,
handheld jigsaw, paint, LEDs, and
microcontrollers

Rotten Cocktails/Boy Robot, 200
Album design with custom letteri
for Boy Robot/City Centre Offices
Berlin
Hand-drawn in ink, digitized, 3-D
rendering

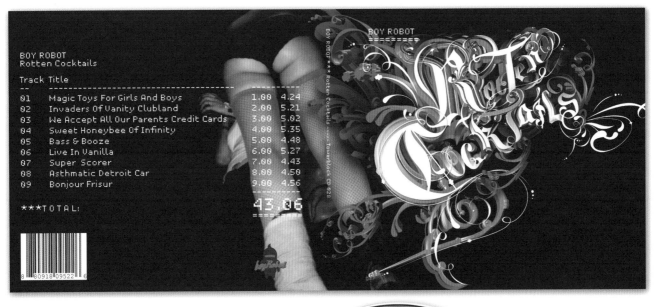

BOY ROBOT
Rotten Cocktails

Track Title

01	Magic Toys For Girls And Boys	1.00	4.24
02	Invaders Of Vanity Clubland	2.00	5.21
03	We Accept All Our Parents Credit Cards	3.00	5.02
04	Sweet Honeybee Of Infinity	4.00	5.35
05	Bass & Booze	5.00	4.48
06	Live In Vanilla	6.00	5.27
07	Super Scorer	7.00	4.43
08	Asthmatic Detroit Car	8.00	4.50
09	Bonjour Frisur	9.00	4.56

★★★TOTAL: 43.06

8 80918 09522 6

written & produced by Hans Möller and Michael Zorn
design by StrangeAttractors.com
mastered by Lupo at D+M
mailto: boyrobot@web.de

BOY ROBOT
*Rotten Cocktails
=========
Distributed by Baked Goods (UK), info@baked-goods.com and Morr Music (rest of the world),
info@morrmusic.com
C+P CITY CENTRE OFFICES 2005, cco@city-centre-offices.de, www.city-centre-offices.de
TOWERBLOCK CD 028

ⓒ

+++Hugs & kisses:

Bex, Peter, Thaddi, Mark, Mario, Eva, Ryan & Cateljne, Shlom, Simon,
Howie, Miles, Paul, Jan, Kai, Martin, Thomas, Uwe, Britta, the Möller Family,
the Audionaut Clan, Erik, Fredrik, Bonke, Alu, Matz, Erik F, Crissie
and all other friends in Uppsala, Berlin and the rest of the Universe.
===

Tape Gallery's Georg Schnitzer, Christoph Priglinger, and Oliver Laric were born in Siberia.

MATILDA TRISTRAM

WWW.LOVELYCAT.CO.UK

By day, Matilda Tristram works in a basement as an animator. By night, she draws comics, plays records in iniquitous London lairs, buys wigs on eBay, writes music reviews, e-mails her friends, and thinks about tidying her bedroom. After graduating with a bachelor of arts in illustration from the University of Brighton, she set up Afootbooks, a small press and publishing company, to sell and print mini comics. Recent publications include *Gum*, *Having Babies Is Easy*, and *The Pearl Necklace*. Matilda studied in London, Brighton, Minneapolis, and Berlin, and has drawn pictures since the very moment she was born.

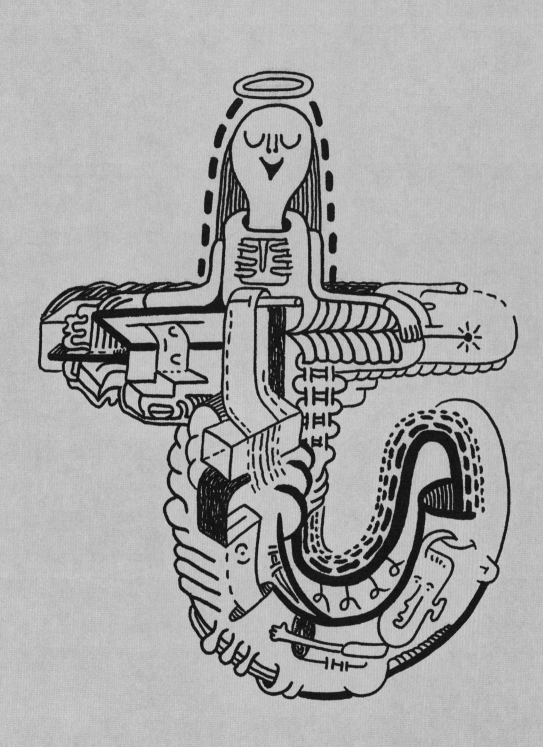

Fifty T-shirts, 2005
Custom T-shirts
Colored tape

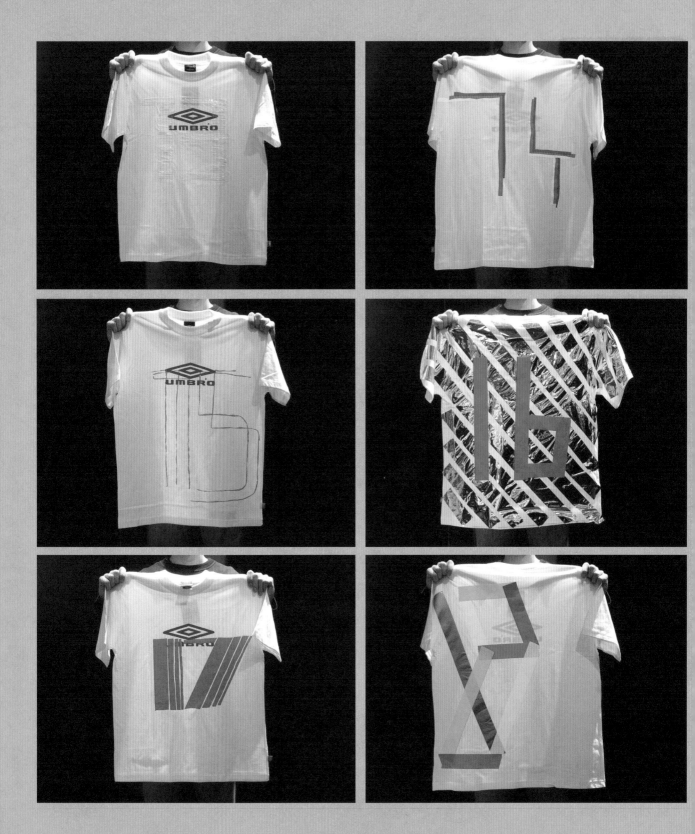

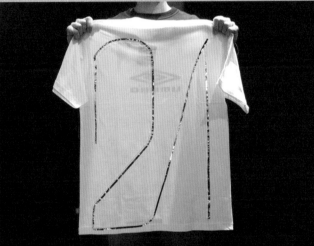

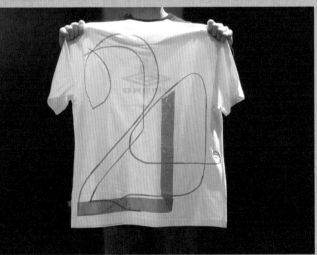

Forget about the Sugar, 2005
Postcard
Pen and computer

It's Alright I know my Limits, 200
Drug Beats and Hippies, zine
Pen on paper

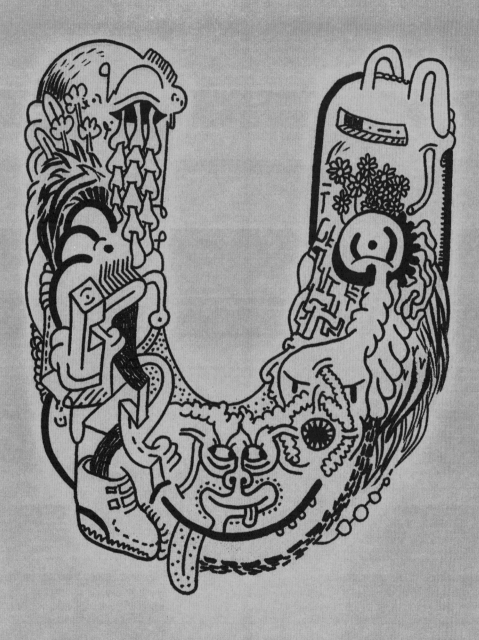

Currently, Leon Vymenets is working in Toronto
as a freelance artist. Some of his passions
include strummin' on his ukulele and sharing his
darkest secrets with his Siamese cat, Dima.

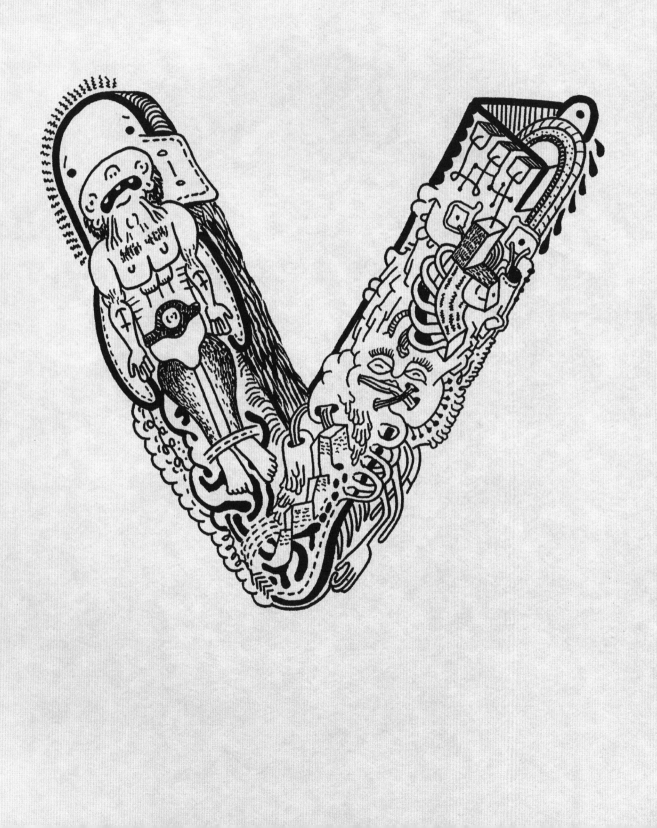

Ragga Muff, 2005
Sketchbook Page
Pen on paper

Man Obey Woman, 2005
Sketchbook Page
Pen on paper

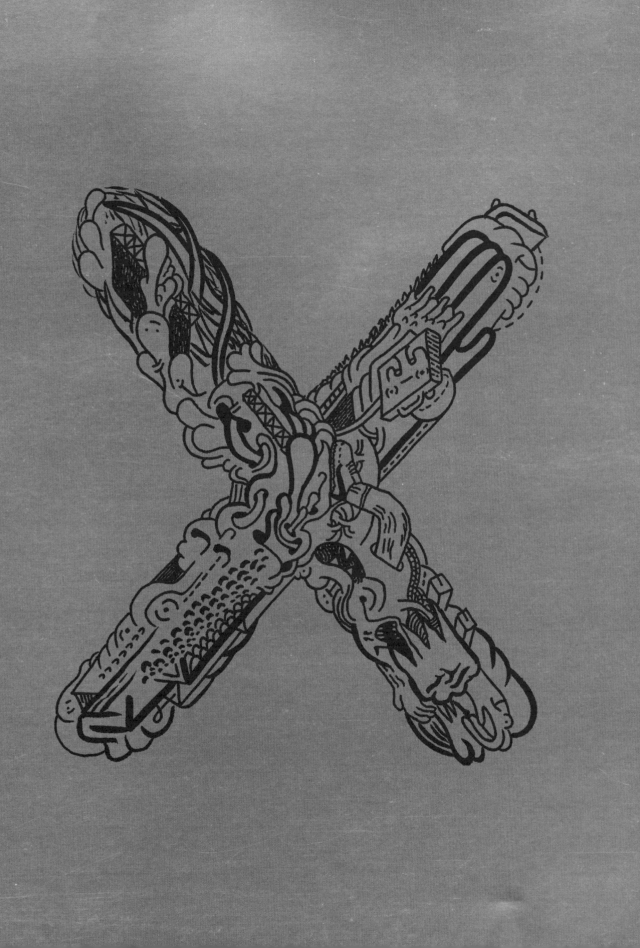

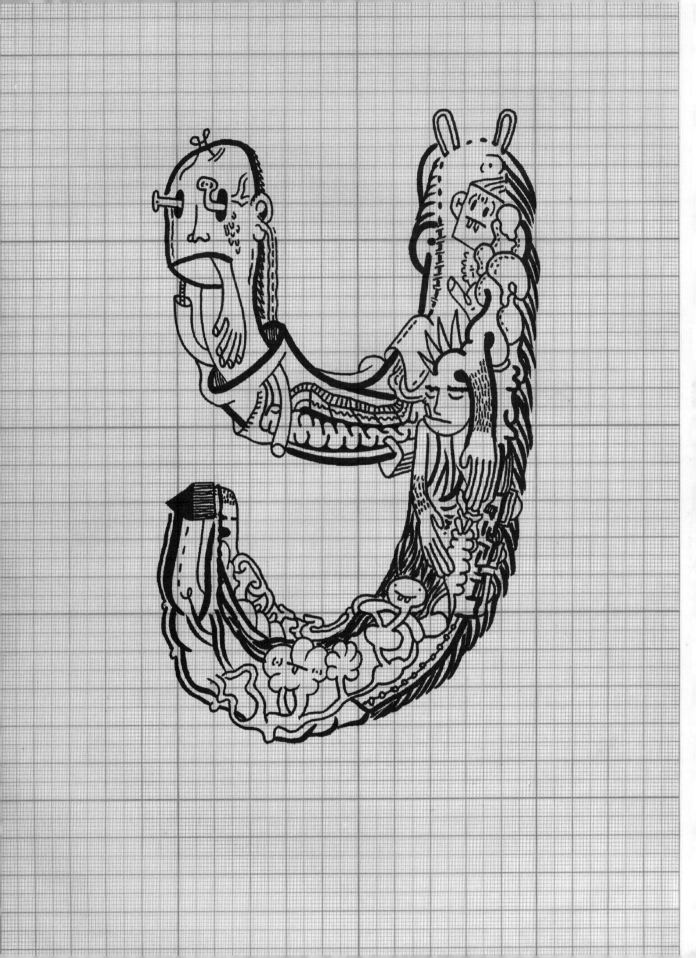

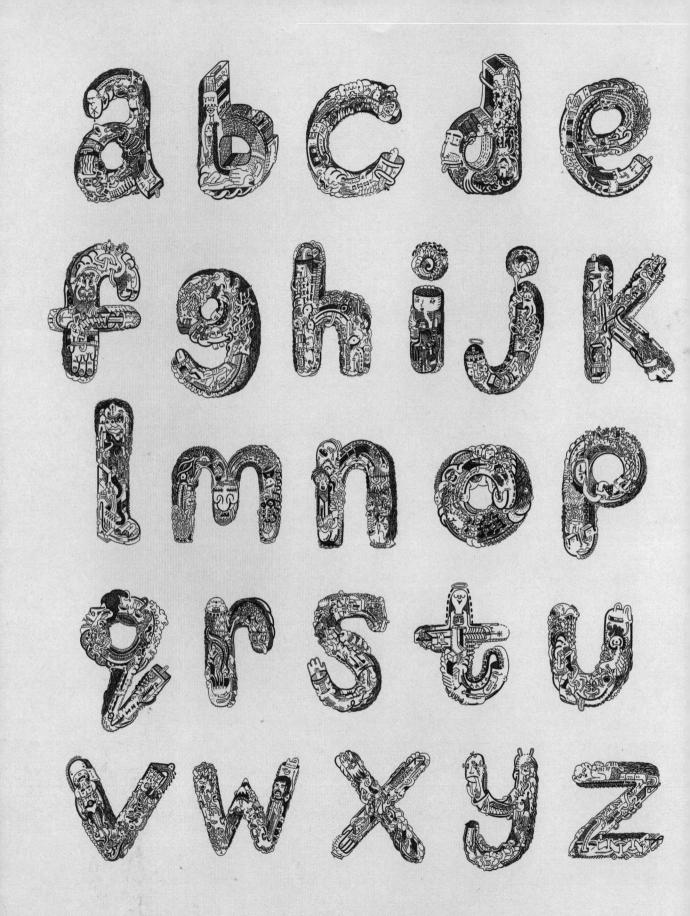